TAMING THE BEAST

TAMING THE BEAST

Can We Bridle the Culture of Corruption?

Robert Osburn Jr

Wilberforce Press
St. Paul, Minnesota

Wilberforce Press
Published by Wilberforce Press, PO Box 130551 | St Paul MN
55113

Requests for permission to reproduce material should be sent to
Permissions,

http://wilberforceacademy.org

Illustrations by Virginia Thao.

   Osburn Jr., Robert
   Taming the beast: Can we bridle the culture of corruption?/
Robert Osburn Jr.
   ISBN: 1530699770
   ISBN-13: 978-1530699773

Printed on acid-free paper.

Printed in the United States of America.

Dedicated to my international student friends, past and present

Table of Contents

Acknowledgments

Ponder carefully the names on this page. In my mind's eye, they are heroes that dared to advise, critique, analyze, parse, debate, caution, encourage, and otherwise help shepherd into print a book that has been sorely needed for a long time.

They, like me, cast a long glance at their world, and find it terribly wanting. It is a world not meant to be this way, that is, a world with terrorism, inequality, callous indifference, poverty, fragmented families, wars, epidemics, sorrows of all kinds and corruption. They volunteered to read a portion of this book that represents one of the very first to offer a new perspective —a biblical perspective —on a shattering reality all too common in most parts of the world.

In one way or the other, they read part or all of this text. Their efforts have collectively summoned forth a text that would be far shabbier were it not for their generous investment of time: Karin Thomas, Andy Larson, Hyunjun Kim, Rinto Dasuki, Colin Gan, Ameido Amevor, Ricardo Sandcroft, Emmanuela Nyam, Thangboi Haokip, Abbel Joseph, and Jianyong Liang. If I have left out someone's name, I would feel so sad. *Mea culpa.*

There are five people, however, whose valiant efforts deserve special attention. Steve Ferguson challenged me to write this book, both because of the lack of good writing on the topic and the hunger for something substantive, yet readable. Stacey Bieler labored over the text as much as any volunteer, and made recommendations that have seen the light of day and made it a better book. Dear friend Michael O'Connor has the sharp eye of not only a proofreader, but also the savvy mind of a thinker who asks the questions that need to be asked. He, too, will see the fruit of his labors inside the covers of this book. Scott Rank, thank you for the pleasure of working with you and producing this book in what has been, in fact, a genuine global effort. Last but not least, my wife of 40 years has cheered, prodded, and offered a listening, loving ear when the mind and spirit thinned out amidst the birth pangs of this book. Thank you, Susan.

Of course, none of those mentioned will agree with everything written here, nor should they. All errors of fact or interpretation are mine and mine alone.

For His Glory!

Robert Osburn

Preface

Has someone asked you, perhaps more times than you can count, for a bribe? Has someone threatened to destroy your business, your home, or perhaps your life unless you pay a bribe?

Like billions of others on our planet, you must feel like corruption is a beast that needs taming. Like a very aggressive dog, it is mean, intimidating, and it makes you wish you lived in a different neighborhood. Or even in a different nation.

The beast needs taming. But, who will do it? Our leaders can't, and, most often, they won't (since corruption often serves their interests).

Tempting as it may be to think otherwise, our often-corrupt leaders also share the same image of God. They are *not* beasts. And, furthermore, as we will see in Chapter Two, the Bible teaches that we, like our leaders, are also corrupt sinners in need of an incorruptible Savior.

Courageous civil society campaigners inspire us to tackle the beast of corruption and put it in its place. However, the beast is big and hungry, as we will see in Chapter Six.

I am also very confident as a Westerner that Western leaders can't solve the problem in your country, either.

Only one leader throughout all of history has been able to tame the beast: Jesus of Nazareth, revered by most people in our world, and worshiped by those who follow Him. He does it in a subtle way by converting us from greed to grace, and in more obvious ways by inspiring us to courageously resist, expose, and love those who serve the beast, but who may secretly want to escape the beast's bloody grip.

So, this is a book of 12 tales (made-up stories) that unmask God's judgment against corruption. They can be read separately or consecutively. Each answers a unique question about corruption but all, in one way or the other, show why and how we need to join Jesus in taming the beast. Occasionally, as in Chapter 11, the metaphor may change (corruption as cancer, for example), but the beastly reality is still the same. Jesus' unchanging power is the only power that can conquer a deeply embedded evil like corruption.

Let's find out how to tame the beast, shall we?

Introduction

In these still-early years of the twenty-first century, people around the world are revolting against bribery and corruption. From Anna Hazard of India to the World Bank[1] to Xi Jinxing of China,[2] the battle against corruption unites people of virtually all ideologies, worldviews, religions, and philosophies. Not only do the citizens of the People's Republic of China believe that their single greatest contemporary challenge is corruption, but the same can be said of the citizens of countries stretching from parts of Latin America though Africa and on to most of Asia.

Together, we wonder: Can we tame this beast, the global scourge of corruption?

Surprisingly, Christians have not been as prominent in this battle as they have been in battles over slavery, sex trafficking, and abortion.[3] Why is this the case? The answer to that question involves another: "Where do the most-published Christian thinkers live?" They live in Western countries where corruption and bribery are not prominent issues. Therefore, when they write about the Bible's teaching about how we are to live, they conveniently and predictably ignore what it says about corruption and bribery.

If we have any hope of vanquishing the corruption we see all around us, the time has come to discover what the Bible, the word of God, says about bribery and corruption. Among theologians, a book like this is sometimes called a "biblical theology" of bribery and corruption because it tries to make sense of the meaning of the biblical passages about bribery and corruption. It also tries, in a modest way, to connect that biblical teaching to larger ideas and concepts that make a difference for every one of us.

Beware: What the Bible says about bribery and corruption may surprise you. For one thing, while corruption is usually defined as the dishonest attempt by those in power to enrich themselves at other's expense,[4] we discover in the Bible something even more stunning about corruption: It spoils, damages, and destroys those people and societies that it affects. It may privately enrich a few, but will damage and destroy many.

1

Introduction

There is a second thing the Bible teaches about corruption that should shock you: It makes the claim that each of us is corrupt in our very core. This shocking and disturbing news means that we are not only completely out of sync with God's original design for us as human beings, but that our lives spread destruction. Each of us not only damages creation but we also damage human society. And what we once enjoyed in the bright sunlight must be reserved for secret and dark places. Whereas we were born to love one another, now we use our skills and positions to diminish and rob each other. That is why the word *corruption* was often used by English Puritans (1550 to 1675 AD): It conveyed the shocking effects of sin.

Every one of us are born with a sinful predisposition to be out of sync with our original design. But what does that have to do with corruption? As I will explain in this book, we were designed by God to do two things: 1) protect the rest of His creation through its wise management; and 2) produce those products and services that make human life, and the rest of life on the earth, flourish.[5] When sin entered the human race, the first human beings not only became corrupt but their lives took a U-turn: Instead of protecting, they started to destroy and to damage what God had made, and instead of producing, they started fighting over limited resources. Instead of living utopian lives in the proverbial Garden of Eden, they became defaced, diminished, and deranged human beings.

So, the system of corruption, including bribery, extortion, and fraud, began when humans realized that they could get their needs met by stealing from others instead of loving them, as God intended from eternity.[6] Individuals and ethnic groups discovered that, instead of producing and protecting, which was God's strategy to meet their needs, some of them met their needs through bribery, extortion, and fraud.

But, what is it about bribery that is so wrong? Are we in favor of it if we can collect bribes, and against it if we are the ones paying bribes? If we are made in the image[7] of a God who cannot be bribed, then we have very good reason to object to bribery and all other forms of corruption.[8] But, why would that be the case? All the other so-called deities that inhabit the world seem to welcome offerings and sacrifices and other means of, shall we say, bribing them to do what we want. That is the point: God is not like all the other small deities that demand payments in order to accomplish what we want. Instead, the true God who made the Universe gives to human beings what they don't deserve. He refuses to conduct illicit transactions with us. He only acts in our best interests, while bribery and corruption are designed to serve the interests of those with power.

But, who are those with power? Who benefits from this system of corruption that attracts the anger of most people who live upon our earth? We learn in this book that bribery and corruption are big business because power has been centralized in government bureaucracies created by nation-states. This modern world is designed to make powerful those who act as representatives of government, whether government ministers, parliamentarians, customs officers, police authorities, or whatever. Because they possess power, they have the capacity to rob people through corruption. But, one reason they have so much power is due to something premodern: the belief that spirits must be paid to accomplish our wills. This old animistic perspective hangs on among a great number of the world's inhabitants, and so when they meet government employees, it is almost as if they are meeting the shamans and witch doctors who control access to the world of spirits. So, we discover that something premodern—the belief in a world of spirits that inhabits the created world—is married to the modern, bureaucratic nation-state.

But, as we will see in Chapter Ten, there is yet a fourth factor: the influence of Western higher education on elite students from around the world. Tragically, at the very time when leaders of integrity are needed to combat the ballooning levels of corruption, many Western educators have abandoned the search for truth in favor of something that seems so much more concrete and relevant: ending the imbalance of power and wealth between the rich and the poor. As worthy as that goal may seem, it has diminished the desire to pursue the good, the true, and the beautiful. Having diminished the moral status of corruption, one more barrier against corruption has effectively vanished.

That means that corruption is a big problem that won't go away easily. It is a problem that weaves together personal evil with systems or structures of evil. In other words, the problem involves very personal decisions that we make on almost a daily basis. For example, should I pay that bribe the policeman is demanding? Or, should I dilute the milk I am selling with water so that I can make more money from unsuspecting customers?

But, when the problem of corruption goes beyond, or transcends, any one of us, then it becomes systemic, or structural. That happens when we realize that there are unstated expectations for bribes, or when we realize that different groups in society pressure people to act corruptly, or when we realize that our country's economy is directly influenced by the thievery of corruption.

While the book may depress us because it exposes the evil of corruption, in the end we should be hopeful. Christ's ultimate victory is assured, but until then, pastors and others can teach in the way that I describe in Chapter Twelve:

> Remind followers of Christ that corruption belongs in their *past* lives, never in the present. They should teach that corruption violates our dignity as God's image bearers and violates our human purpose as virtuous protectors and producers. Finally, they can show that only through the sinless Son of God, Jesus Christ, is God able to create in each of us a new heart that is oriented toward the virtue of love for neighbors and away from the vice of corruption.

Humor in a Serious Book about Corruption

Our goal in this book is to discover what the Bible says about bribery and corruption, with a view to showing how bribery and corruption defaces and diminishes our humanity. But this somber, sober message will be couched within a deep under-current of wry humor that, as you will see, threads its way in and through the chapters that follow, albeit with a mixture of deep sorrow on occasion.[9]

Grin often with the knowing smile. You just may utter under your breath, "Oh, yes! So I'm not the only one who thinks that giving bribes under those conditions makes buffoons out of all of us!" For some of us, humanizing the less-than-human aspects of our existence (such as the house fly whom you will meet in the judge's chambers in Chapter Eight) helps cast a humorous glow over the enormity of injustice, especially when there seems little that we can do, humanly-speaking.

Corruption *is* a serious topic, and so our occasional attempts at humor are vaguely reminiscent of earlier fables, which teach profound moral lessons under the guise of humor. 19th century American preacher Henry Ward Beecher once said, "A person with a sense of humor is like a wagon without springs. It gets jolted by every pebble on the road." The relentless, daily demands for bribes, threats of extortion, and the specter of fraud are those pebbles. Hopefully, the stories embedded in these chapters will teach profound moral lessons that have their roots in the Bible, God's Word, while also utilizing dismissive humor that helps us keep perspective.

A Caution

The risk with a book like this—a collection of fictional stories, interviews, reports, and other narratives—is that one might think that writing in such a style diminishes the truthfulness of biblical teaching. After all, "one fiction deserves another, doesn't it"?

If I thought, along with many Western academics, that the Bible is a mere fable, full of concocted stories and morality tales designed to nudge the human race toward morality and a naive belief in God, then I would have long ago dropped this project. But, to do so would have betrayed a refusal to explore *why* Western societies, so often guided by biblical teaching, have been spared the worst of corruption. It would also have betrayed a similar refusal to imagine that those same guiding forces and ideas might have a similarly liberating impact in other societies around the world. As so many of the readers of this book will know, there are few solutions outside of what the Supreme God tells us. Science can uncover the *nature* of reality, but it has no capacities to tell us *how* to live our lives, both individually and in society.

Therefore, this book aims to expose the pernicious, globe-spanning evil of corruption in the light of Biblical teaching and Christian theology. The result, I hope you will agree, is far more substantial and profound than any of us ever imagined.

A Note about the Interviews

As you will also discover, each chapter stands alone, usually either as a story, a confidential report, or as an interview. While you should know that the stories and the confidential report (Chapter Eleven) are fictional, so are the interviews.

As a reader, it might help you to understand the psychology of both the interviewer and the interviewee (at least in the chapters where they are present). They are very curious, and often have a lively interest in what others have learned. In a world created by God, but diminished by sin, truthful realities emerge from under the humblest of rocks. And so mystics, moles, and mice make clever observations about the most devious of human behaviors (and corruption usually involves boatloads of deviousness!). The interviewer is usually eager to discover how Jesus Christ redeems this terrible problem, and so he will at times seem both stubborn and silly. But, know that he really is looking for answers (probably just like you).

Government Officials

You will notice that the narratives in this book sometimes poorly reflect on government officials. It is not because working in the government is inherently evil. Rather, it is the observation that working in government often brings out the worst in its employees, perhaps because, as Lord Acton so famously said, "Power corrupts, and absolute power corrupts absolutely."

Every one of us has, however, had a pleasant experience with a government employee, but not because government employment engenders pleasantness. Rather, we have reason to believe that some internal transformation has taken place inside the employee, rendering him or her a person of grace, service, and sincerity, as well, one hopes, of professionalism.

We also know that many government employees are themselves innocent victims of the "system" of corruption that thrives in their nations and even internationally. To our shame, as you will see in Chapter Eleven, Christian churches are sometimes centers of corruption. In some Western countries, a saying goes, "Those who live in glass houses shouldn't throw stones," and that saying most certainly derives from Jesus' teaching that one shouldn't judge others until you have examined your own blind spots.[10] Christians do well to be humble.

God loves to see His creatures flourish and reproduce in abundance[11]. Why won't leaders do likewise? Instead, many leaders seem to embrace a crimped, narrow view of reality that assumes only a finite amount of resources rather than ever-enlarging horizons and possibilities.

Chapter Summaries

In the interests of clarity, I end each chapter with an outline of the key points embedded within the chapter. This not only reinforces, in a more traditional way, the biblical themes relating to bribery and corruption, but it also offers a systematic summary.

Study Questions

Educators are increasingly aware that helping people genuinely *learn* involves the strategic use of questions. After all, a great deal of Jesus' teaching was embedded within questions. Thus, each chapter ends with a short list of questions designed to enable groups to explore the meaning of biblical teaching about bribery and corruption, but also its application to our daily lives.

Don't Forget to Read the Appendix

What the Bible teaches about bribery and corruption is one thing; it is another matter to apply that teaching successfully to our every day lives, especially when our sinful natures, government bureaucracies, postmodern ideas, and ancient shamanistic practices conspire to keep us trapped in the culture of corruption. Thus, the Appendix offers ideas, many of them tested amongst groups of undergraduate and graduate students from around the world, for limiting or putting a stop to bribery and corruption. Please let us know about your own experiences at

Introduction

www.wilberforceacademy.org/corruption.

Now, dive into the book, and meet our varied cast of characters (a mouse, a housefly, a couch, the underside of a table, a weigh scale, etc.), all with much to teach you about a biblical perceptive on bribery and corruption. And above all, let us learn to follow the One who gives us the best hope for conquering the beast.

NOTES

1. World Bank (2013). *G20 Leaders Anti-Corruption Commitments.* Downloaded on 12/9/14 from http://star.worldbank.org/star/sites/star/files/g20_leaders_com mitments_compilation_sept_2013.pdf.

2. Macabe Keliher & Hsinchao Wu, "How to Discipline 90 Million People," *The Atlantic,* April 7, 2015, http://www.theatlantic.com/international/archive/2015/04/xi-jinping-china-corruption-political-culture/389787/.

3. Robert Osburn, "Under the Table? Why Bribery and Corruption Must Be Rescued from the Shadows and Given Prominence in Global Evangelical Social Ethics." (Paper delivered to the Midwest Regional meeting of the Evangelical Theological Society, Chicago, IL, March 2012).

4. e.g., Susan Ackerman, *Corruption and Government: Causes, Consequences, and Reform* (New York: Cambridge University Press, 1999).

5. Genesis 1:26-28. *Then God said, "Let us make man in our image, after our likeness. And let them have dominion over the fish of the sea and over the birds of the heavens and over the livestock and over all the earth and over every creeping thing that creeps on the earth."*

> *So God created man in his own image,*
> > *in the image of God he created him;*
> > *male and female he created them.*
> *And God blessed them. And God said to them, "Be fruitful and multiply and fill the earth and subdue it, and have dominion over the fish of*

the sea and over the birds of the heavens and over every living thing that moves on the earth."

6. Matthew 22:21. *And whatever you ask in prayer, you will receive, if you have faith.*

7. Genesis 1:26. *Then God said, "Let us make man in our image, after our likeness. And let them have dominion over the fish of the sea and over the birds of the heavens and over the livestock and over all the earth and over every creeping thing that creeps on the earth."*

8. Deuteronomy 10:17. *For the LORD your God is God of gods and Lord of lords, the great, the mighty, and the awesome God, who is not partial and takes no bribe.*

9. In the English language, the term "wry humor" is used to describe humor that is subtle and rather under-stated in order to make the point that something is wrong.

10. Matthew 7:1-5. *"Judge not, that you be not judged. For with the judgment you pronounce you will be judged, and with the measure you use it will be measured to you. Why do you see the speck that is in your brother's eye, but do not notice the log that is in your own eye? Or how can you say to your brother, 'Let me take the speck out of your eye,' when there is the log in your own eye? You hypocrite, first take the log out of your own eye, and then you will see clearly to take the speck out of your brother's eye."*

11. Genesis 1:28. *And God blessed them. And God said to them, "Be fruitful and multiply and fill the earth and subdue it, and have dominion over the fish of the sea and over the birds of the heavens and over every living thing that moves on the earth."*

CHAPTER ONE

The Mouse in the Anti-Corruption Office

"Why do we condemn corruption?"

"Ouch!"

My toe had just slammed into some unknown obstacle in the Office of the Government Minister for Anti-Corruption Affairs. I was there in the dead of night when only the mice (and the occasional rat) scurry back and forth in the never-ending search for food. Since I had arrived the day before on a flight from the States, I was wide awake. Two o'clock in the morning here was more like six o'clock in the evening back home.

How did I manage to slip into this prominent government office under cover of darkness? After all, I had to pass by multiple guards and military patrols. Did I slip them money? (Be honest: You're thinking that I did exactly that!)

Well, have you heard about the three guards who surrounded the tomb of Jesus after He was buried there? Somehow, miraculously, the guards' eyes were blinded, and the Risen Savior disappeared before they had any idea that His body was gone.[1] What about the earthquake that suddenly popped open the doors of the Apostle Paul's jail in Philippi?[2] Or, consider Peter's miraculous escape from prison. He passed countless guards who were completely unaware that he was escaping with the help of an angel.[3] These stories should give you clues about how I entered the Anti-Corruption Affairs office, and, of course, departed unmolested by guards.

I was here to "shine a light" on what should have been the most transparent[4] office in the nation. My mission was to interview the one soul (I use the term "soul" very loosely) who knew a lot about what took place in this office during daylight hours. In order to expose evil, especially a deeply - embedded evil like corruption, we journalists have to look for some of the most creative and well-hidden sources. Even mice.

Word had come to my desk back in America that an exceptionally well-studied mouse was the one "soul" willing to discuss damning evidence about the goings-on of the office. What I cared about was the fact that his daytime haunt was in a very narrow and dark space just behind a bookcase near the minister's desk. The mouse heard everything, *even when he was "sleeping." Much of what he overheard remains to this day a carefully guarded secret that will only see the light of day when my interviews with him are published.*

What I can *share from our interviews over several nights is shocking. And disturbing, as you will no doubt agree.*

Sometimes it takes a tiny rodent to tell the truth we humans would rather ignore.

****

Tell me, Mouse, how long have you been here.

My late mother moved us here about eight months ago, which is equivalent to about 20 years of human life. The food and accommodations are the best our family has ever seen. I've taken responsibility for the extended family since her life ended about five months ago when a rogue cat found its way here.

Sorry to hear about your loss. Now, the reason that I'm here is to find out what you've overheard about the government's big plan to eradicate corruption.

(Laughter.)

What's so funny?

(More laughter.) Oh, please…
(The mouse doubles over—or, is it under?— in uncontrolled laughter for another 15 seconds, and then composes himself.)

Okay, you must be ignorant about the fact that—and I have this on good authority amongst the mouse fraternity, which is a worldwide organization—many government offices like this are a sham: They pretend to fight corruption among government officials, but they often actually protect it and sometimes promote it. And when corruption is attacked, it is often a cover for a power struggle.

You human beings can be devilishly creative!

Tell me more.

Just the other day, I overheard a phone conversation where the Anti-Corruption minister said, "Sure, Mr. President, I'll meet with Jack—he is a local journalist who likes big stories—and give him all he wants to know about Jing's corrupt activities." Well, I'm no dummy. I know what's going on. Jing and the president have been at each other's throats to see who can outrank the other. It's a power struggle, nothing more, nothing less.

Well, I've heard about this sort of thing. Tell me more about in-fighting amongst powerful people and corruption in this office.

The office helps protect leaders who are corrupt, sometimes by giving them tips about those who are trying to expose their corruption, often arranging meetings where the officials decide how they are going to cover up corruption.

The Mouse in the Anti-Corruption Office

Of course, in public they claim to be ending corruption. Have you heard about your fellow journalist, John Githongo in Kenya? He was actually quite serious about his job as anti-corruption czar, only to discover that he was being used to cover up the corruption of more powerful officials. Githongo barely escaped to Great Britain, and even there some homegrown thugs went after him.[5]

This is grisly stuff.

You said it! Wait a minute...Have you ever read a Bible? You know, the Christians' holy book that claims to reveal God's intentions for humans like you. Being a Westerner, you must know something about it. From what I hear, it's getting more attention all the time, and it has everything to do with the relative absence of corruption in countries that were historically influenced by Protestant Christianity. Even the minister in this office claims to attend church every Sunday.

What about the Bible?

I would think that a smart journalist like you would pay attention to it.

Touché!

If you look at the Bible, you will discover that the core idea behind the Bible's use of the word *corruption* is that which destroys, ruins, or spoils. Think of a nice banana. What happens when you pick it and then fail to eat it weeks on end? It spoils. The same thing happens with a piece of meat that is not immediately eaten or refrigerated or somehow salted to preserve it.

So, the first reason why humans deplore corruption is because it spoils societies and makes them worthy for God's judgment. The first reference to corruption in the Bible is in Genesis 6:11-12.[6] The people of Noah's era were described as violent and corrupt: "Now the earth was corrupt in God's sight, and the earth was filled with violence. And God saw the earth, and behold, it was corrupt, for all flesh had corrupted their way on the earth."

They were literally destroying themselves and everything around

14

them. The Hebrew word for corruption (*shachat*) was used in the Old Testament to refer to injury, ruin, and spoilage. In the New Testament, the Greek word for corruption, *phtheiro* (and related words),[7] means to decompose, or be destroyed through a decomposing process. The word, or those related to it, is used nine times in the New Testament [8]

According to the Bible, corruption destroys what was once healthy and vibrant through a process like that when bacteria infect food and spoil it. You humans and your societies are spoiled by corruption, which was first identified with gross moral perversion and violence. Any way that you look at it, corruption kills.

We humans tend to think that you mice spoil things for us. But, you are saying that, biblically, the real problem is a corrupt dynamic at the core of human societies!

Exactly.

How do you respond when something valuable spoils? You grieve that something so wonderful has been lost! In Genesis 6:6 God grieved over the massive self-infected human ruin that results from sin: "And the Lord was sorry he had made man on the earth, and He was grieved in His heart" (NASV).

Consider these other examples from the Bible. The great priest Ezra who led the people of Israel in mass repentance after their exile in Babylon reminded them of the original command given to the Jewish people when they conquered the Promised Land: "The land you are entering to possess is a land polluted by the corruption of its peoples. By their detestable practices they have filled it with their impurity from one end to the other."[9] Evil, destructive practices had created a culture where the Canaanites had become morally perverted. God commanded the Jews to take it over so that it would become a productive and flourishing land where moral order prevailed.

Consider the ancient city of Sodom, famous for its evil, corrupt culture. Would God completely destroy the city? Abraham's nephew had settled in Sodom, and so Abraham had a personal stake in seeing judgment averted. He asked God if He would completely destroy the city if only a small group of righteous people lived within it. The answer, mercifully, was "No." In the end, God destroys the city, but only after rescuing Lot's righteous family from that thoroughly corrupt city that destroys not only those within it, but everything around it.[10]

You have my attention! Corrupt societies earn God's wrath. That's scary.

The last reference to corruption in the Bible is Revelation 19:2: "He (God) has condemned the great prostitute who corrupted the earth by her adulteries. He has avenged on her the blood of his servants." The prostitute, identified in Revelation 18 as Babylon, very likely referred to Rome, the luxuriant and corrupt city at the heart of the 1st century AD Roman empire. Massive commercial activity, abundant wealth, and vibrant cultural activity, when cut off from worship of the living God, could not cover up the corrupt soul of Roman civilization. God judged it, and by 500 AD it was no more. Cultural spoilage, all fostered from within, earned God's judgment on Rome.

So, I get the idea that corruption is a destroyer that spoils and ruins societies. How does it affect God?

We have some really intelligent mice who have been reading the Bible, and they tell me that it says that God cannot be bribed.[11] Absolutely never. He is grieved by corruption, but never complicit in it. A bribe not only violates His moral character, but since His power is supreme, no one can use their power or purse to get Him to do what they want. On all levels, God simply cannot be bribed to do the will of His creatures!

Hmmm! So what's so unique about a God who refuses to take bribes?

You're not from around here, are you? Maybe you've read or heard something about animism, the idea that spirits animate the entire physical world—rocks, trees, rivers, etc. A basic rule is that spirits expect to be bribed—paid off, if you prefer—in order to do the bidding of humans. If one of your neighbors feels envy over

16

the fact that you are getting wealthy because of hard work and smart investing, they go to a witch doctor and bribe him to contact a local spirit to destroy your wealth-making abilities. The spiritual world demands bribes before showing concern for humans; God shows humans grace and kindness even when we have nothing to offer but our broken lives.

Do you comprehend this? You look a little stunned. *(Quiet laughter)*

(Mild coughing) I never thought that the spiritual world had anything to do with messy stuff like corruption.

We mice have been studying you humans for some time. Some of you, especially people who grew up in the West, have difficulty connecting daily life problems with the spiritual world. Some of you have a big wall that separates the spiritual from everyday experiences.

Okay, I admit that Westerners have really forgotten how to connect daily life to God.

The fact that God cannot be bribed points to another reason why corruption has to be condemned: It destroys impartiality, which is the hallmark of true justice. Note how Deuteronomy 10:18 connects God's refusal to take bribes (expressed so clearly in the previous verse) to His impartiality in the administration of justice. [12]

You mean God's impartiality explains the Hebrew concept of justice?

My dear friend human friend, you have just struck gold! (I think that's what you say when someone has a great insight.) Because Israelite culture was profoundly shaped by the character of God, impartiality was central to the Jewish idea of justice. In other words, those with money and power can't simply purchase justice! This idea of impartial justice was carried over into Christian societies.

The Mouse in the Anti-Corruption Office

Since you are a Westerner from a society shaped by the Christian heritage, I hope you appreciate that fact, because it means more than you can imagine!

I'm stunned. Here I am talking with a mouse in the middle of the night in the office of the minister for anti-corruption, and I'm being given a history lesson that I should have been taught in our schools!

Sometimes it stuns our mouse community to see how humans can be so incredibly ignorant about their heritage!

Anyway, we're discussing why you humans condemn corruption, and we note that the second reason corruption deserves condemnation is because, as a God who cannot be bribed, He is absolutely impartial. Jewish and Christian societies were profoundly shaped by that idea of impartial justice.

You know how to get my attention, don't you, mouse?!

Besides the gross moral evil and God's impartiality, there is a third reason why corruption deserves the condemnation it receives: It completely and thoroughly undermines your humanity and your two-fold human purpose. You were designed to protect God's creation and to produce the goods, institutions, and services that make societies flourish. You humans have a two-fold purpose that is built right into the essence of your humanity, but most of you don't even know it!

Well, why do you say that?

It sounds like you have never thought about this.

Well...

Look at Genesis 1:26.[13] What does it say about being a human person? The first thing it says is that humans are made in God's image, in his likeness. You humans look like God, at least in terms of your capacities to reason, create, and make moral judgments. As mice, we have nothing like this.

18

Humans deplore corruption both because it violates God's character and because it violates the character of human beings. Your character reflects his character like a face in a mirror reflects the one who is pictured in the mirror. He simply hates bribes, and so do you, because you are made like him.

But the second thing that the verse says is that human beings are to "rule" over the rest of creation, whether birds, domestic animals, or creeping animals like me. Yes, I am admitting the blunt truth that your purpose, in part, is to rule over me.

Well, that is a nice thought. Even though we may be your masters, you mice seem to know how to escape our control!

We try our best! *(The mouse smiled deviously.)*

But, let's talk more about your two-fold human purpose. God designed you to rule, or, as it says in Genesis 1:28, to exercise dominion over the rest of creation.[14] That's a responsibility that befits royalty, don't you think?

I like the way you are talking!

Your dominion means two things. First, you must protect God's creation by wisely stewarding what God has made, like a good manager working on behalf of the rightful owner of a business, for example.

Well, I hope you don't expect me to protect you mice when you spread diseases and eat human food...

No need to worry. We mice know that we get out of control too often, and you humans have to control us, sometimes with lethal measures, I am sorry to say. I do appreciate the fact that tonight you are not undertaking such lethal action with me!

You are giving me a lot of good intelligence, mouse, and so I have no reason to harm you.

Besides protection, humans are also supposed to produce those things that make human life and the rest of creation flourish. That list is almost endless: laws, vehicles, buildings, books, schools, businesses, agricultural produce, computers, garbage collecting facilities, toilets, furniture, the list goes on and on and on. It's really too much for my mouse brain to think about!

I am learning a lot tonight, mouse. But, what does this two-fold human purpose—protection and production— have to do with the reasons why we humans hate corruption?

Corruption of any kind undermines your human capacities to care for creation and to create what humans and the rest of creation need. Think of all the hours that you spend each week trying to avoid and circumvent corrupt officials. Those hours are wasted hours, lost hours! Instead of thinking how to do a better job of protecting and producing, you had to spend them fruitlessly.

As a mouse, I have to say that your situation, as human beings, looks tragic. You have so much potential to do so many good things for all creation, but you let rampant corruption dampen and diminish all the good that could be done!

Here I am: A human being who is supposed to rule over you, my dear mouse. But, in fact, you tell me the painful truth that corruption steers us far away from our purpose. And to think that a lowly mouse has to tell the truth about the human race!!!

I know it hurts, and I want to say that I feel your pain...

So, to review: The question is "Why does corruption deserve condemnation?" The first reason is because it spoils human societies and makes them worthy of God's judgment because they lead to gross moral evil and violence. The second is that corruption violates the very character of a God who cannot be bribed and who is impartial in His justice. The third reason you condemn corruption is because it distorts and diminishes your ability to fulfill your human purpose as wise stewards and intelligent creators and producers.

But, there is a fourth and final reason: You humans are really very, very corruptible beings yourselves.[15] It's not just that as whole societies you are corrupt, but you are individually corrupt. This is called "original sin" in the Bible, and it means that hard-wired into humanity, owing to Adam and Eve's first sin, is the predisposition to rebel and be autonomous from God.

Wait a minute. I don't pay bribes...well, almost never...so how can you say people like me are corruptible?! Excuse me, but what gives a contemptible creature like you the right to say things like this about me and those like me?

Ahem... I didn't mean to offend you, my friend. I realize that I touched on a very sensitive issue, and, since I am a mouse, I have to be careful what I say. Some people may be offended. I'm only reporting what the Bible says. Look at the Bible's record of human evil, and look at all the evil things that people do today. Look at what Jesus says about the evil in human hearts. You have to conclude that humans are individually corrupt. One of your great religious movements of the past—they were called the Puritans—always spoke and wrote that humans are corrupt. Their prayers, their letters were full of this kind of language. They had a very dismal, but I think highly realistic perspective on the human problem.

Remember, my home is in the Office of the Minister for Anti-Corruption!

Here's what really convinces me that humans are corrupt: Almost all the political leaders who claim they will wipe out corruption become corrupt themselves. Amongst the international fraternity of mice, we exchange intelligence about those who run for political office on the promise to fight corruption. They almost inevitably become just as corrupt as the leaders they replace. It's like a fixed law.

King Jotham was one of the Jews' finest kings, ruling about 2800 years ago over the southern kingdom of Judea. Even after valiantly serving his people, the Bible says, "the people...continued their corrupt practices."[16] You can't blame bad leadership for their problem. This was a problem rooted in the hearts of Jewish citizens at that time in history. You humans would love to blame your leaders, but sometimes the problem is inside each of you.

The Mouse in the Anti-Corruption Office

The Apostle Paul indicted the human race in Romans 1 for its massive corruption.[17] In the final verse (32), Paul declares that humans know that evil and corruption deserve death, but, still, they keep marching forward in their evil, corrupt ways. If it weren't for the redemptive hope that God has offered through Jesus Christ, no human would have a chance.

Do you ever wish you were a mouse like me?! We are just mice, we are not corrupt!

I've got to think about this. I admit I don't like some of what you are saying, not just because you are a mouse, but because I don't like to think of myself as corrupt, or, in biblical language, sinful. And, then, the idea that God is incorruptible... Almost every leader I know thinks of himself like a god, and yet he demands bribes. He expects pay-offs before he pursues public justice.

Here is an illustration that will help you to see how these things are connected. Think about the board games you humans love to play, Monopoly for example. The creator of the game sets up rules that the players are to follow. The creator of that board game is long since dead, and so he couldn't care less whether you follow the rules. But, what happens when someone breaks the rules? Some very competitive people are likely to become very angry, and then conflict breaks out.

Corruption works that way: When humans violate the design that God built into His creation, they only make themselves more miserable through fighting.

It's one thing to say that humans deplore corruption because they are made in Gods image, and that God, by definition, cannot be bribed. It's yet another to say that humans also deplore corruption because it violates everything about their original design. But, the problem is that ever since the First Couple ate the forbidden fruit, humans have been inherently corruptible.[18] They are now wired for the very things that oppose God's character.

American pastor John Piper captured the terrible reality of the human condition when he said, "Sin will take you farther than you want to go, keep you longer than you want to stay, and cost you more than you want to pay." It's a tough thing being a human—

with your sinful corruptibility—living in a corrupt world.

I feel like I want to curl up and die... Being human is really very painful.

I can see that I have penetrated deeply. Believe me, I am not trying to hurt you any further than you already are. You humans are constantly after us mice, but inside me I feel embers of compassion for you and the human race.

Humans and their societies were not designed to automatically spoil, but they are steadily afflicted and diminished by this reality. It really shows the desperate nature of the human condition, painful as it is for me to say this so directly to you.

(Silence for about 10 awkward minutes as the journalist slips behind a bookcase in the dimly lit nighttime office. He blows his nose several times, coughs, and finally re-emerges with reddened eyes.)

I had no idea that our conversation would be so incredibly enlightening, and, at the same time, so painful.

To watch the evil that goes on in this office—supposedly the center of the fight against corruption in this country—sometimes takes away the breath of mice like me. The fighting, the yelling, the clever, hideous laughs, the constant, nonstop lies that pass for press releases, the utter waste of resources... It all just seems so unnecessary. At the end of the day, concludes the brilliant University of California legal scholar John Noonan, bribes are contrary to being human.[19]

But, there may be hope! If God is who He says He is, and He is not only all-powerful, but completely good, is it possible that He may have created a solution? I don't mean some kind of pill to alleviate the symptoms—a sort of "aspirin" for the human race. I mean a more permanent and durable solution that only God could design.

I hope so, I hope so.

I am sorry that I need to end this conversation now. Before the minister comes in a few hours from now, I need to finish collecting food for the rest of the day. Please do stay in touch, won't you?

Indeed. It will be a long time before I forget this conversation.

SUMMARY

1. Corruption, in the biblical languages of Hebrew and Greek, refers to a process of spoilage and ruin.
2. We condemn corruption because it:
   a. Spoils societies and makes them worthy of God's condemnation because of gross moral evil
   b. Undermines God's character as an impartial judge (impartiality is the hallmark of true justice)
   c. Undermines our humanity and the two-fold human purpose of protecting God's creation and producing the goods, institutions, and services that make societies flourish
   d. Dwells in each of our lives due to original sin
3. Cause for hope: Does God have a solution?

STUDY GUIDE

1. Why did God destroy both the ancient pre-Flood world in which Noah and his family found themselves (Genesis 6), as well as the cities of Sodom and Gomorrah (Genesis 18-19)? Why did Rome suffer a similar fate around 500 AD (as predicted in Revelation 19:2)?
2. How is your society similar to and different from these societies that suffered God's judgment?
3. How does engaging in corruption undermine our dual human purpose to protect what God has given us and to produce what humans need? Give a concrete example.
4. What are some evidences for the claim that all humans are personally corrupt due to original sin?
5. Decide how you will share with one other person

something you have learned in answer to the question
"Why do we humans condemn corruption?"

6. What practical idea for "Taming the Beast" (found in the Appendix) will you and your group deploy as a result of reading this chapter?

NOTES

1. Mt. 27: 62-66. *The next day, that is, after the day of Preparation, the chief priests and the Pharisees gathered before Pilate and said, "Sir, we remember how that impostor said, while he was still alive, 'After three days I will rise.' Therefore order the tomb to be made secure until the third day, lest his disciples go and steal him away and tell the people, 'He has risen from the dead,' and the last fraud will be worse than the first." Pilate said to them, "You have a guard of soldiers. Go, make it as secure as you can." So they went and made the tomb secure by sealing the stone and setting a guard.* Mt. 28: 4. *And for fear of him the guards trembled and became like dead men.* Mt. 28:11-15.*While they were going, behold, some of the guard went into the city and told the chief priests all that had taken place. And when they had assembled with the elders and taken counsel, they gave a sufficient sum of money to the soldiers and said, "Tell people, 'His disciples came by night and stole him away while we were asleep.' And if this comes to the governor's ears, we will satisfy him and keep you out of trouble." So they took the money and did as they were directed. And this story has been spread among the Jews to this day.*

2. Acts 16:25-28. *About midnight Paul and Silas were praying and singing hymns to God, and the prisoners were listening to them, and suddenly there was a great earthquake, so that the foundations of the prison were shaken. And immediately all the doors were opened, and everyone's bonds were unfastened. When the jailer woke and saw that the prison doors were open, he drew his sword and was about to kill himself, supposing that the prisoners had escaped. But Paul cried with a loud voice, "Do not harm yourself, for we are all here."*

3. Acts 12:1-11. *About that time Herod the king laid violent hands on some who belonged to the church. He killed James the brother of John with the sword, and when he saw that it pleased the Jews, he proceeded to arrest Peter*

also. This was during the days of Unleavened Bread. And when he had seized him, he put him in prison, delivering him over to four squads of soldiers to guard him, intending after the Passover to bring him out to the people. So Peter was kept in prison, but earnest prayer for him was made to God by the church.

Now when Herod was about to bring him out, on that very night, Peter was sleeping between two soldiers, bound with two chains, and sentries before the door were guarding the prison. And behold, an angel of the Lord stood next to him, and a light shone in the cell. He struck Peter on the side and woke him, saying, "Get up quickly." And the chains fell off his hands. And the angel said to him, "Dress yourself and put on your sandals." And he did so. And he said to him, "Wrap your cloak around you and follow me." And he went out and followed him. He did not know that what was being done by the angel was real, but thought he was seeing a vision. When they had passed the first and the second guard, they came to the iron gate leading into the city. It opened for them of its own accord, and they went out and went along one street, and immediately the angel left him. When Peter came to himself, he said, "Now I am sure that the Lord has sent his angel and rescued me from the hand of Herod and from all that the Jewish people were expecting."

4. Organizations that reveal their finances and operations to the public are described as "transparent" because one can observe their operations.

5. Michela Wrong, *It's Our Turn to Eat: The Story of a Kenyan Whistle-Blower* (London: Harper Perennial, 2010).

6. *Now the earth was corrupt in God's sight, and the earth was filled with violence. And God saw the earth, and behold, it was corrupt, for all flesh had corrupted their way on the earth.*

7. The word *cognate* is used in English to describe words that derive from the same root word.

8. (The translations appear in *italics*): I Cor. 3:17 (*destruction*), I Cor. 15:33 (*corrupt*), II Cor. 7:2 (*corrupt*), II Cor. 11:3 (*corrupt*, or *lead astray*), Eph. 4:22 (*corrupt*), II Pt. 2:12 (*destroy*), Jude 1:10 (*corrupt*, or *destroy*).

9. Ezra 9:11. *Which you commanded by your servants the prophets, saying, 'The land that you are entering, to take possession of it, is a land impure with the impurity of the peoples of the lands, with their abominations that have filled it from end to end with their uncleanness.'*

10. Genesis 19:14. *So Lot went out and said to his sons-in-law, who were to marry his daughters, "Up! Get out of this place, for the LORD is about to destroy the city." But he seemed to his sons-in-law to be jesting.*

11. Deuteronomy 10:17. *For the LORD your God is God of gods and Lord of lords, the great, the mighty, and the awesome God, who is not partial and takes no bribe.*

12. *He executes justice for the fatherless and the widow, and loves the sojourner, giving him food and clothing.*

13. *Then God said, "Let us make man in our image, after our likeness. And let them have dominion over the fish of the sea and over the birds of the heavens and over the livestock and over all the earth and over every creeping thing that creeps on the earth."*

14. *And God blessed them. And God said to them, "Be fruitful and multiply and fill the earth and subdue it, and have dominion over the fish of the sea and over the birds of the heavens and over every living thing that moves on the earth."*

15. Psalm 53:3. *They have all fallen away; together they have become corrupt; there is none who does good, not even one.* Isaiah 1:4. *Ah, sinful nation, a people laden with iniquity, offspring of evildoers, children who deal corruptly! They have forsaken the Lord, they have despised the Holy One of Israel, they are utterly estranged.* Romans 3:23. *For all have sinned and fall short of the glory of God.*

16. II Chronicles 27:2. *And he did what was right in the eyes of the LORD according to all that his father Uzziah had done, except he did not enter the temple of the LORD. But the people still followed corrupt practices.*

17. Romans 1:18-32. *For the wrath of God is revealed from heaven against all ungodliness and unrighteousness of men, who by their unrighteousness suppress the truth. For what can be known about God is plain to them, because God has shown it to them. For his invisible attributes, namely, his eternal power and divine nature, have been clearly perceived, ever since the creation of the world, in the things that have been made. So they are without excuse. For although they knew God, they did not honor him as God or give thanks to him, but they became futile in their thinking, and their foolish hearts were darkened. Claiming to be wise, they became fools, and exchanged the glory of the immortal God for images resembling mortal man and birds and animals and creeping things. Therefore God gave them up in the lusts of their hearts to impurity, to the dishonoring of their bodies among themselves, because they exchanged the truth about God for a lie and worshiped and served the creature rather than the Creator, who is blessed forever! Amen.*

For this reason God gave them up to dishonorable passions. For their women exchanged natural relations for those that are contrary to nature; and the men likewise gave up natural relations with women and were consumed with passion for one another, men committing shameless acts with men and receiving in themselves the due penalty for their error.

And since they did not see fit to acknowledge God, God gave them up to a debased mind to do what ought not to be done. They were filled with all manner of unrighteousness, evil, covetousness, malice. They are full of envy, murder, strife, deceit, maliciousness. They are gossips, slanderers, haters of God, insolent, haughty, boastful, inventors of evil, disobedient to parents, foolish, faithless, heartless, ruthless. Though they know God's righteous decree that those who practice such things deserve to die, they not only do them but give approval to those who practice them.

18. Genesis 3:1-7. *Now the serpent was more crafty than any other beast of the field that the LORD God had made. He said to the woman, 'Did God actually say, 'You shall not eat of any tree in the garden'?' And the woman said to the serpent, 'We may eat of the fruit of the trees in the garden, but God said, 'You shall not eat of the fruit of the tree that is in the midst of the garden, neither shall you touch it, lest you die.'' But the serpent said to the woman, 'You will not surely die. For God knows that when you eat of it your eyes will be opened, and you will be like God, knowing good and evil.' So when the woman saw that the tree was good for food, and that it was a delight to the*

eyes, and that the tree was to be desired to make one wise, she took of its fruit and ate, and she also gave some to her husband who was with her, and he ate. Then the eyes of both were opened, and they knew that they were naked. And they sewed fig leaves together and made themselves loincloths.

19. John Noonan, *Bribes* (New York, Macmillan, 1984), 706.

CHAPTER TWO

The View from the Purse

"How does corruption affect people?"

The View from the Purse

Whether made of leather, cloth, or plastic, purses are bags into which their owners stuff all kinds of personal items, including personal identification, credit cards, and money. Imagine the experience of being a purse: constantly carried about at the side or on the shoulder of your owner, stuffed with personal items, opened and closed frequently, and dropped in corners or chairs when not in use.

I managed to coax a purse hanging on the shoulder of a wealthy South American businesswoman to tell us her story. I wanted to learn what it is like to be a purse that is frequently used in mostly petty corruption, especially the paying and receiving of bribes. The most interesting thing about the purse's story, however, is what it reveals about how people experience corruption.

The purse will show us that both those who suffer and benefit from corruption are its tragic victims. Corruption, after all, is terribly destructive to society at large (see, for example, Chapter Nine and the devastating impact of corruption on economies). Corruption also hurts every single person in society. The shame, the calculating spirit, manipulativeness, and the sense of being imprisoned haunt those who live in highly corrupt societies where bribes and extortion are daily realities.

And now, the purse's revelations about the experience of corruption…

****

I enjoy intimacy with my owner, who treasures me, not because of what I am but because of what I contain. I put up with the indignity of being folded, creased, hugged, jerked open, latched shut, thrown, and dangled, all because I carry precious cargo. On occasion, with my owner angrily grasping the handle, I've been slapped across her husband's head. (Why her angry outbursts and his sullen response? She seems to honor her diamonds more than the man she married some years back. Meanwhile, he seems insensitive toward her need to talk about the government officials who keep their grubby hands extended until she deposits the requisite bribe.)

Anyway, let me tell you about my cargo. To fully appreciate my perspective, you have to know that my cargo hold is usually dark and sometimes I choke for air. That means you *can* suffocate inside me, but that is not my real worry.

What troubles me are those regular occasions when my owner opens me to remove currency so that she can pay bribes. A businesswoman who must chase down government permits, she has little choice but to seduce all sorts of public officials with the slim, crisp currency bills—maybe you call them *cash*— that form the bulk of my cargo. When she disgorges the bills, I feel the sense of relief that comes after my sides have been stretched to the breaking point. The currency bills (poor things) almost scream, "So now you are tossing us into the hands of another money-grubbing official. We're passed around like prostitutes!"

Sometime I think those currency bills exaggerate. I even feel sorry for some of the officials who demand them from my owner. Did you know that some of them haven't been paid their salaries for over six months? These officials—often lowly officials who work as police or customs and border agents—have hungry families back home. Their paymaster—he's often called the minister of finance, or a similar title— manages government cash. Top officials may need a few million for their next shopping trip in Monaco (or some other expensive destination reserved for the super-wealthy of the world), and, so, lowly officials don't get paid while top officials jet to Europe or the USA.

At home, children of lowly officials ask, "Daddy, when are you going to get us enough food so that our stomachs don't ache when we go to school?" There is something very evil about all of this.

"But, why object?" you say. "Those bills get things done!" As a purse in close contact with the currency I carry, I hear the stories, I see the injustices. This matters; real lives are at stake.

Another challenge facing my owner are the suppliers who taint and otherwise cheapen the wholesale products they sell her. In their own ways they are as corrupt as the government officials who demand bribes. It is the price of business, after all, or so they say.

For a mere purse, I have a very uncomfortable task: telling the truth about the painful human experience of corruption. I'm really trying to tell a story that also drinks deeply from the well of biblical thought. What I discover, both from experience and the sacred scriptures, is that humans who engage in corrupt activity are haunted by shame, heartlessness, a sense of vulnerability, and a feeling of powerlessness.

Shame

The shame, or deep embarrassment, associated with corruption is shared. When it comes to dealing with public officials, utility companies, doctors, or suppliers, my owner slinks her hand inside me as if on a secret mission. Her hand slithers in and out like a snake while she turns her body so that others can't see what she's doing. Suddenly, currency bills magically disappear from her hands and into someone else's closed fist.

What is the secret she is hiding? I, of course, know all about the illegal transaction—the *bribe*—that has taken place, but she wants to hide what she has done from other human beings. Is she overcome with secret shame at having to bribe someone? Why does this simple act, repeated hundreds of millions of times each day around the world, cause ragged, deep emotions to emerge from and then disappear again into the darkest places of the human soul?

Her shame was also shared by the one who received her bribe. One day when she tried to pay her utility bill, the clerk kept telling her that the amount wasn't right. My owner fixed her sharp blue eyes on the clerk and stared quietly. That's when I noticed beads of sweat forming on his forehead. "He must be new at this job," I thought. I knew what he wanted, she knew what he wanted, and shame lurked beneath the surface.

At that delicate moment I realized that bribe takers and bribe givers share a common experience originally forged in the Garden of Eden long ago. Genesis 3 recounts how sin rocked the beautifully innocent world of the naked First Couple who enjoyed a shameless existence[1]. Immediately following Eve and Adam's taste of the forbidden fruit, they scurried behind a bush, afraid to be seen naked[2]. They were suddenly terrified that God would see them, exposed and vulnerable. Their physical nakedness was, it seemed to them, a declaration: They were emotionally and spiritually naked and helpless.

That look of shame must be similar to the shame that creeps across the faces of those who, today, play for their personal advantage at public expense (which is what most corruption is about).

Professor Noonan (who was quoted near the end of the first

34

chapter of this book) discovered that bribery is universally shameful:

> In no country do bribe takers speak publicly of their bribes, or bribe givers announce the bribes they pay. No newspaper lists them. No one advertises that he can arrange a bribe. No one is honored precisely because he is a big briber or a big bribee. No one writes an autobiography in which he recalls the bribes he has taken or the bribes he has paid.[3]

He has also exposed the subtly superior attitudes of Westerners: "It is often the Westerner with ethnocentric prejudice who supposes that a modern Asian or African society does not regard the act of bribery as shameful in the way Westerners regard it."[4] Though I am but a lowly purse, I am persuaded by Prof. Noonan's declaration that shame is a universal experience when one gives or takes bribes. The impulse to hide, to disguise, to mask: It's all a version of the First Couple's same frantic attempt to cover themselves with leaves and other vegetation. Shame is unnatural.

What is natural is to be open, undisguised, and unafraid. The natural condition of a human being reflects the words of Jesus when he told His followers to "let your light shine before others, so that they may see your good works and give glory to your Father who is in heaven."[5] The only things that should be done in secret are prayer, being generous,[6] and, having sexual relations with one's spouse. For the follower of Christ, shames keeps God from the glory He deserves while keeping humans entangled in that very shame they so dislike.

Heartlessness

With tears flowing, Jeremiah weeps in Lamentations 4:3: "My people have become heartless like ostriches in the desert"(NIV). This tragic portrait of how social evil turns humans inward upon themselves (to use St. Augustine's image of the damage done by sin) reveals the coldness and cruelty in corrupt societies. Corruption makes you heartless, and neighbors lose love for neighbors, shopkeepers for customers, and pastors for their flocks. Human beings, made in the image of the Triune God where Father, Son, and Holy Spirit have eternally loved one another, [7] become worse than animals when corruption reigns.[8] What is the end result of the callous heartlessness generated by corruption? "The tongue of the nursing infant sticks to the roof of its mouth for thirst; the children beg for food, but no one gives to them."[9]

I remember a Southeast Asian student who spoke to my owner of his great anxiety about having to go back home and face the customs officials at his nation's capital airport. He wanted to love his homeland, but cold demands for bribes upon re-entry made him feel heartlessly used. Rather than honest, open-hearted joy in living, humans must coldheartedly plot and plan how they will satisfy the telephone repairman, the medical doctor, the ticket seller, and, yes, the customs official, each of whom demands a bribe before they offer their services. These folks come not to serve, but to fleece and to empty purses like me into their heartless pockets.

Heartless people measure others by what you can do for them, not what they can do to serve you with courtesy, generosity, and thoughtfulness. Less than a decade ago, one state governor in the USA[10] coldly sold the US Senate seat of a man who would later become a US president.[11] Amazingly, he had earlier bragged that he would clean up corrupt politics in his state. When humans coldly measure what others can do for them, they not only reduce others' humanity, but they also reduce their own.

Vulnerability

The shamefulness and callousness that infect corrupt societies is further compounded by the sense of vulnerability, or weakness and helplessness, that corruption causes. Humans are created to be affectionate, caring, loving beings who seek each others' best interests.[12] But sin deforms and diminishes the human capacities to live as they were intended, with the result that humans also experience vulnerability.

The mark of the serpent in Gen. 3:1 was his "craftiness." Satan personified, he was a clever master at discovering the woman's weaknesses for the purpose of entrapment. He posed a question subtly designed to make her question God's goodness.[13] He not only challenged God's integrity, but suggested that disobeying God would have a hidden reward.[14]

As a purse, I've seen this exploitation of human vulnerabilities time after time! Those who demand bribes are masters at spotting weaknesses—at national borders, when businesses are launched, when licenses are needed, when medical care is urgently requested, and at all the other occasions when humans need help and assistance. I'm most often opened at just such times: In goes her hand, out comes a wad of bills that suddenly disappears into the grubby claws of someone who is supposed to render "service" (a word related to the concept of a "servant"). That person might better be labeled the "master of vulnerability."

I think Job (after whom a book of the Bible is named) must have felt similar vulnerability when his so-called friends, acting as counselors, told him that he suffered because he sinned. Broken by their constant attacks on his character, he finally declared (more out of a sense of extreme weakness, rather than as a declaration of truth) that corruption was "my father."[15] At a time of extreme vulnerability, it almost seemed like terrible evil was his closest confidante (though the opposite was the case).

I'm the sort of purse that feels the pain of others, and, believe me, I feel my owner's pain and anger at times like these when she is made to feel vulnerable before corrupt suppliers and government officials. She might as well be naked like Eve. When bribes are demanded before services can be rendered, humans feel exposed and bare as if they were being pawed over by lusty men with their prostitutes.

Why do you think that national leaders like Jokowi[16], the president of Indonesia since late 2014, can so openly stroll among his people? Why did Indonesians flock around him and honor him like few national leaders have ever been honored? Because, for the first time in Indonesia's history, they had a leader known for never demanding bribes while also resisting corruption.[17] People felt secure around him, not vulnerable. They believed they could trust him.[18]

Powerlessness

Powerlessness compounds the shame, the heartlessness, and the vulnerability that dominates the human experience of corruption. When I feel my owner clutch me very, very hard, then I know she feels powerless, as if she is becoming someone's slave. Those demanding her bribes want her to know they are the masters who can demand her possessions and even her life if she does not pay up. And so she holds me firmly, as if to declare that she, too, can master something or someone.

You humans long to be free. That is the theme of most of your favorite films and television shows. You want to be able to walk down the street, manage your farm, conduct business, and raise your family without someone breathing down your neck to control you.

I understand that the mouse you met in the Office of the Minister for Anti-Corruption Affairs (Chapter One) said that all human beings are corrupt. He meant that all humans have an inner desire, one they often struggle to resist, to disobey God and to hurt other human beings. Well, the woman who was first seduced by the crafty serpent in Genesis 3 gave birth to a son who was born with the same corruptibility. One day, Cain became very angry with his brother Abel, who was also born with the same sinful corruptibility.

Cain's problem, said God, was that he was vulnerable to letting sin become his master, his slave driver: "It desires to have you, but you must rule over it."[19]

How do I, a mere purse, understand the human condition? Yes, I observe it carefully but I also know what the Bible teaches. Genesis 1:26-28 declares that God made human beings in his image (how I wish that I could have that privilege!).[20] He designed humans to wisely rule (protect and produce) the rest of God's creation for its good, God's glory, and human flourishing. God designed humans to be royalty who make the earth a wonderful place to live.[21]

When humans fell into sin (Genesis 3) they not only became guilty before God and lost their loving relationship with Him, but they also became slaves to sin (Romans 6). When God warns Cain that he must rule over sin lest it rule over him, the stakes were enormous. Sadly, Cain let sin rule him, and he ended up murdering his innocent brother.

Corruption diminishes human beings, whether by causing shame, vulnerability, heartlessness, or powerlessness. You look almost pathetic and small when you refuse to serve one another unless there is money under the table. It's so sad to see you humans powerless, caged in, enslaved, victimized by yourselves and your sin.

Can corruption be mastered? Are humans inevitably the slaves of a system that extorts and demands bribes? You feel powerless when faced with these demands, much as Cain must have felt powerless. But humans have a choice, a moral choice, because corruption and bribery is a morally bankrupt system that compromises human morality.

When Cain gave into sin's mastery, he not only did not flourish, but he also suffered the fate of a sojourner, cast upon the lonely landscapes of a thousand failed dreams. He suffered a "curse," the very opposite of a blessing. Honor was lost. Status was lost. Even his vocation (growing crops) failed him, according to the text. All the props were lost, all because of a failure to master sin, the corruption within. Unless societal corruption, including bribery and extortion, is mastered, it will master humans and they will sometimes pay the ultimate price.

Choices do matter, and it seems abundantly obvious that mass resistance to demands for bribes will bring the system to heel. It must be mastered, it must be treated and tamed, or it will, at great cost, tame humans and shrivel your societies.

An Alternative to Shame, Heartlessness, Vulnerability, and Powerlessness

The shame associated with bribery is magnified in cultures where honor and shame control social life. Honor must be preserved at all costs, and shame must be avoided at all cost. And yet, honor-shame societies are overtaken with bribery and corruption. Is there any hope?

Those willing to consider following Jesus Christ discover that he disarmed shame and took away its terrifying powers when he died upon a cross on the edge of Jerusalem some 2000 years ago. Hebrews 12:2 says that Jesus, "the founder and perfecter of our faith, who for the joy that was set before him endured the cross, *despised the shame*, and is seated at the right hand of the throne of God."

The phrase "despised the shame" means that, as a sinless sacrifice, Jesus refused to let His crucifixion, a Roman method for producing maximum shame and shock upon a citizenry, define the nature of his death. As the sinless Son of God, He willingly endured punishment for the sins of all humans.

Human beings will always feel shame, as well as heartlessness, vulnerability, and powerlessness, whenever there is bribery, extortion, and general corruption. But, that shame does not have to permanently define you, if you are willing to embrace the fact that Jesus was made a sacrifice for your sins.[22]

Note also that Jesus was focused on "the joy set before Him." At the very moment of extreme injustice, what was Jesus joyfully anticipating? Because He was fully God, He anticipated the many billions of people who would become His followers. He knew they would be liberated from the very shame, heartlessness, vulnerability, and powerlessness that corruption creates. Imagine His joy when you become one of His followers: You no longer have to be defined by corruption; instead, you replace it with love for your neighbor that mirrors the love God has for you. And you will, in the process, also experience His joy, even in a world of injustice![23]

As a purse that has been used in far too many corrupt transactions, I look forward to that! My master will be happier, and the currency inside me will enter the hands of those who justly deserve it. "Blessed are those who act justly, who always do what is right!"[24]

SUMMARY

1. Humans who engage in corrupt acts experience:
    a. Shame, or deep personal embarrassment.
    b. Heartlessness.
    c. Vulnerability.

      d. Powerlessness.

2. Rather than letting shame define His unjust crucifixion, Jesus was joyous instead.
    a. He loved us by being sacrificed on our behalf so that we can love God and each other.
    b. Joy can replace the negative feelings associated with corruption.

STUDY GUIDE

1. Have you ever reflected on the human experience of corruption? Why or why not?
2. What does the experience of Adam and Eve (as recorded in Genesis 3:8-24) reveal about the shame associated with bribery?
3. Describe an experience with corruption that involved either heartlessness, vulnerability, or powerlessness. How does Jesus Christ respond to those experiences?
4. Ponder Hebrews 12:1-2 carefully, and imagine Jesus' joy as you follow Him in a world that is often unjust. What do you learn from your reflections?
5. What practical idea for "Taming the Beast" (found in the Appendix) will you and your group deploy as a result of reading this chapter?

NOTES

1. Genesis 2:25. *And the man and his wife were both naked and were not ashamed.*

2. Genesis 3:7-8. *Then the eyes of both were opened, and they knew that they were naked. And they sewed fig leaves together and made themselves loincloths. And they heard the sound of the Lord God walking in the garden in the cool of the day, and the man and his wife hid themselves from the presence of the Lord God among the trees of the garden.*

3. John T. Noonan, Jr., *Bribes* (New York: Macmillan, 1984), 702-3.

4. Noonan, 703.

5. Matthew 5:16.

6. Matthew 6:1-6. *Beware of practicing your righteousness before other people in order to be seen by them, for then you will have no reward from your Father who is in heaven. Thus, when you give to the needy, sound no trumpet before you, as the hypocrites do in the synagogues and in the streets, that they may be praised by others. Truly, I say to you, they have received their reward. But when you give to the needy, do not let your left hand know what your right hand is doing, so that your giving may be in secret. And your Father who sees in secret will reward you. And when you pray, you must not be like the hypocrites. For they love to stand and pray in the synagogues and at the street corners, that they may be seen by others. Truly, I say to you, they have received their reward. But when you pray, go into your room and shut the door and pray to your Father who is in secret. And your Father who sees in secret will reward you.*

7. John 17:24. *Father, I desire that they also, whom you have given me, may be with me where I am, to see my glory that you have given me because you loved me before the foundation of the world.*

8. In Lamentations 4:3. Jeremiah says that, by contrast, *"even jackals offer the breast; they nurse their young."*

9. Lamentations 4:4.

10. Rod Blagojevich, Governor of Illinois (2002-2009).

11. Barack Obama, President of USA (2009-).

12. Philippians 2:4. *Let each of you look not only to his own interests, but also to the interests of others.*

13. Genesis 3:1. *Now the serpent was more crafty than any other beast of the field that the Lord God had made.*

14. Genesis 3:3. *But God said, 'You shall not eat of the fruit of the tree that is in the midst of the garden, neither shall you touch it, lest you die.'*

15. Job 17:14. *If I say to corruption, 'You are my father,' and to the worm, 'My mother' or 'My sister'...* (NIV).

16. His given name is Joko Widodo.

17. Will Jokowi be able to resist what few have been able to resist throughout history? Rarely has a national leader not sought to turn his office into a grand strategy for enriching himself at public expense (corruption).

18. Time will tell whether their trust in him was justified.

19. Genesis 4:7.

20. *Then God said, "Let us make man in our image, after our likeness. And let them have dominion over the fish of the sea and over the birds of the heavens and over the livestock and over all the earth and over every creeping thing that creeps on the earth." So God created man in his own image, in the image of God he created him; male and female he created them. And God blessed them. And God said to them, "Be fruitful and multiply and fill the earth and subdue it, and have dominion over the fish of the sea and over the birds of the heavens and over every living thing that moves on the earth."*

21. If you want to explore this idea, you can learn about the "cultural mandate," a term that the former Dutch prime minister, Abraham Kuyper, created.

22. I John 2:2. *He is the propitiation for our sins, and not for ours only but also for the sins of the whole world.*

23. John 15:11. *These things I have spoken to you, that my joy may be in you, and that your joy may be full.*

24. Psalm 106:3 (NIV).

CHAPTER THREE

The Testimony of the Table

"How do we justify corruption?"

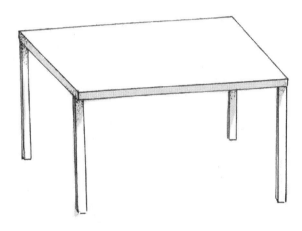

Tables are wonderful inventions where we do all kinds of wonderful things. We serve food on them. We converse across them. Great leaders plot their strategies, for good and for evil, around them. We write on them. Our computers sit upon them. We teach from them. We sell all kinds of products upon them. There is almost no limit to the imaginative ways that human beings use the tops of tables.

But, have you ever thought about the undersides of those tables? Undersides are rarely seen except by small children crawling under tables, or by animals like cats and dogs, or when a table tips over, or when it is carted away. Otherwise, we give no thought to what happens underneath tables, except

45

when we talk about bribery and corruption.

Whether literally or figuratively, most corrupt money passes "under the table." For our purposes, the "underside of the table" is a perfect place to discover the ways that people justify corruption when they know that it is wrong. That's because, as a place of secrecy and darkness, the table's underside pays attention to the many ways that we try to hide our corrupt activity.

A collector purchased our particular table because he treasured its particular design and the rarity of the Berlinia wood that was used to construct it. He later sold it to a wealthy businessman who, in turn, offered it as a "gift" to a government official from whom he sought a contract. So, this table not only has stories to tell about "under the table" deals, but is also itself the product, so to speak, of just such a deal.

Let us read with care the table's story about its underside, and what it reveals about how human beings justify corruption. The Bible's deep concern for human motivations makes this story necessary. It also explains how and why humans pursue corruption with such vigor when they know that it produces, as we saw in Chapter Two, so much shame, heartlessness, vulnerability, and powerlessness.

****

I have appeared everywhere from boardrooms to bedrooms, from dining rooms to manufacturing centers, and have been taken for granted by almost everyone. My topside, known as the "tabletop," is my public side. People employ me for dinners, boardroom deliberations, offices, teaching, and countless other places. When people purchase me, they usually look at my topside, sometimes at my legs, but never at my underside. My topside must always look beautiful and enduring, while my underside is a faithful but quiet servant who is the source of support for my structure as a table.

My underside is, of course, almost completely ignored. In fact, my underside often looks uncared-for: a collection of staples, splashes, stains, and pencil marks made by those preparing to cut the wood that made me a table. Despite its unsavory appearance, my underside witnesses massive amounts of money changing hands. Whereas my attractive topside is where people converse, eat their meals, play games, and sign contracts, the real action seems to happen in my unattractive underside.

The term "under the table" is a code phrase for corrupt transactions almost everywhere around the world, most likely, because people want to hide their illegal transactions. I wish you could witness the clever ways that humans pay bribes without being discovered (or so they think!) by those around them. Here is how one human describes the physical mechanics of passing bribes through handshakes (which are just another form of "under the table" behavior):

> In one type of handshake, the hand is extended toward the person with the palm perpendicular to the floor and the thumb pointing upward in the way that people normally shake hands. When you extend your hand in this way, it is hard to hold money in your hand or to pass money to the other person....In the other type of handshake money can be discreetly passed from one person to the other. The immigration official's palm is parallel to the floor facing upward. The other person's palm is parallel to the floor facing downward with the thumb tucked under the palm. The hands slide past one another pausing briefly for a shake. The immigration official's hand then quickly goes into his pocket or into his desk drawer.[1]

The very important question that we must explore is this: How do people justify, or rationalize corruption, when, in fact, corruption seems to produce such terribly uncomfortable feelings of shame, heartlessness, vulnerability, and powerlessness?

Requiring Universal Participation

One way of justifying corruption is by making sure as many people engage in it as possible. When Eve handed the forbidden fruit to her husband, she was not only sharing with her beloved spouse, but she was making sure that he would join with her in disobedience.[2] In the very first reference to corruption in the Bible, Genesis 6:11-12 says, "Now the earth was corrupt in God's sight, and the earth was filled with violence. And God saw the earth, and behold, it was corrupt, for all flesh had corrupted their way on the earth." God had no choice except to judge the corrupt human race: "I have determined to make an end of all flesh, for the earth is filled with violence through them."[3] The earth had been designed by God as the place where the living creatures he created would flourish under the wise stewardship of human beings who carry God's image in them.[4] Instead, it had become a place of utter chaos, violence, and gross moral evil. Sin's devastating effect was greater than anyone could have imagined when Adam and Eve were royalty in the Garden of Eden.

But, one man walked with God and refused to accept the corruption of the world in which he lived: Noah.[5] In most corrupt societies, most people suspect the person who refuses to engage in corruption. Since this person has no stake in the corruption, they are a threat because they may reveal the corruption to those who can stop it.

Human beings have an amazing capacity for making sure everyone gets involved in evil. The Jewish leaders of first century Israel worked very hard to arouse the crowds with demands that their morally perfect and sinless Messiah Jesus Christ be crucified.[6] In addition to the Jewish leaders, there were many others who were involved with this terrible injustice: the Jewish leader's followers, the Roman political and military leadership and even one of Jesus' followers who had turned traitor.[7]

During the many meals eaten on my topside, I've heard many stories about diligent workers being forced to slow their work so that they don't make their fellow workers look lazy by comparison. I have also heard workers threaten and coerce their fellow workers. In many businesses, workers strike in order to get more pay, benefits, or better working conditions, and while everyone has the right to strike, no one should be threatened if he or she decides not to join the strike effort.

In essence, there is an incentive to get as many people working under the table as possible. That seems to explain why, after the Apostle Paul detailed a list of horrible sins[8] at the end of Romans 1, he wrote, "though they know God's decree that those who practice such things deserve to die, they not only do them but give approval to those who practice them."[9] As I have just indicated, there are very good reasons for getting as many people involved as possible: It spreads the responsibility as widely as possible.

Have you known public officials who insist that their employees participate in the schemes to enrich themselves, such as setting up roadblocks designed to capture those who in the slightest ways violate often unreasonable traffic regulations? Those who refuse are sent to remote locations as punishment for failing to join in.

To refuse to participate in corruption will, in a vast number of government and business offices around the world, tarnish the employee's image in the eye of his or her employer. They make fun of the morally earnest, those for whom integrity is very important. And not only will the employee's prospects be tarnished or made a subject of mockery, but the employee will suffer materially because he or she does not take advantage of the corruption that supplements one's income.

Corruption, while it can make things happen, nevertheless unleashes a fury inside humans, a fury of self-recognition and, for many, of self-revulsion.[10] They want to run from themselves, but they cannot. And so they must join in the system of corruption by using cloaking strategies, disguises, sleight of hand, "meaningful handshakes" stuffed with bills, suitcases strategically abandoned, and stool pigeons.

The system of corruption demands universal participation, and high is the price paid by those who don't participate.

Making Others Share the Blame

Spreading the blame around is another strategy for justifying involvement in corruption. The many dinner table conversations at my table have led to the conclusion that many people involved in corruption will happily transfer their shame onto others. It is the "blame" strategy. After Adam and Eve suddenly felt shame, they then began thinking of how they could blame someone else for their awkward problem. Adam blamed Eve and Eve blamed the serpent.[11] Actually, all three parties were complicit, but no one wanted to take responsibility by themselves.

Sometimes this happens when someone starts blaming a member of their ethnic group: "I did it because my ethnic group expects me, as a government official, to make sure they get some of the government 'cake.'" Whereas shame is a psychological response to corruption, blaming is actually a social response.

While the effort to get everyone engaged in corruption (through requiring universal participation) aims to get everyone secretly under the table, at the same time, the effort to spread the blame around aims to get as many people as possible exposed on the table's topside (accountability). So, corruption has its underside and topside strategy, and as a table I've seen plenty of examples of both.

Rewarding Supporters

There is a third way that corruption is justified or rationalized. A third common justification, as I suggested a few paragraphs earlier, is the claim that their supporters, families, or ethnic groups expect to benefit from corruption. In fact, there is tremendous obligation and pressure to use public funds to reward their supporters and those who raised them in their communities. In other words, these folks pressure otherwise good people to engage in corruption. That is called "social pressure."

Where does this idea—that you must reward those who helped you achieve leadership—originate? It may be a result of the natural gratitude expected of leaders. This shows humility and appreciation that one's rise to power is a function of the love and dedication of one's family and friends. On the other hand, as I have suggested, very often it is a result of the demands made by others. In some societies, to fail to share your wealth is the ultimate expression of selfishness. Who wants to be seen as super selfish?[12]

Frankly, many citizens are in conflict with themselves on this: When a leader from another ethnic group comes to power, they complain about corruption when members of his group get jobs or rewards. But when a leader comes from their own ethnic group, those same people complain when the leader doesn't give them a job or some reward that, otherwise, they would have considered corruption.

You may be surprised to learn that vote buying was accepted behavior in 18th and 19th century England, and that the great Christian social reformer William Wilberforce participated in it, though not without later regrets. That vote buying is completely out of bounds in the United Kingdom today is testimony to the possibility that societies can change and the system of corruption can be strangled. In the case of the UK, it was most certainly a result of the moral and spiritual reformation that resulted from the work of the Wesleyan Christians and the Clapham community with which Wilberforce worked.

The Social Costs of Corruption

All three justifications for participation in the corrupt system—requiring universal participation in corruption, spreading the blame to as many people as possible, and excusing it by virtue of modern political demands to reward supporters—have terrible social costs. They are the dirty, bitter fruits of corruption.

The first cost of participation in corruption is simmering hostility and violence. The first hint of this hostility unfolded in the Garden of Eden. Having all she could want—all the food she needed,[13] immense responsibility for the rest of creation,[14] and, quite literally, a perfect husband[15]—Eve made two fateful mistakes. The first was that she listened to an animal (a snake) over whom she was supposed to be manager ("rule over..," as the text says in Genesis 1:26). The second was to believe the clever lie of the snake (who embodied the Devil), namely, that by eating forbidden fruit, she could achieve the same degree of knowledge as God. After her sin (which no doubt was supported by her husband), Eve found herself in tremendous hostility with the serpent who had deceived her.

He had seduced her to engage in evil (the "underside") and she blamed him for her problems (the "topside"). The guaranteed result was hatred and hostility.[16] While it seems like the "cost of doing business" in so many countries, corruption creates unnecessary enemies. When extorted (a common version of corruption), people feel cheated, and want nothing more to do with the person who dictates at what price they may live.

The hatred and hostility in the Garden of Eden was not limited to Eve and the serpent. The woman's two most important earthly relationships (with her husband and her children) became unnecessarily painful.[17] The pain and hostility even extended to her progeny's relationship with the ground, out of which humans produced those things that helped humanity to flourish.[18]

There is no harmony until the Master (Jesus) masters corruption. Remember that the first reference in the Bible to corruption demonstrated that corruption is associated with violence: "The earth is filled with violence through them."[19] Corruption makes enemies.

Another social cost of corruption is loneliness. The person who refuses to participate in corruption, especially when the practice has been normalized in a society, is easily labeled an "outsider" and made to feel unwelcome. That was prophet Elijah's problem during the reign of King Ahab and Queen Jezebel. Time after time when he spoke the truth about their evil reign, he was forced to hide by himself in order to save his life. He hid by the Cherith brook after warning Ahab that no rain would fall unless Ahab repented of his worship of false gods,[20] and he ran to Beersheba to escape the wrath of Queen Jezebel who was angry that he killed the priests of the false god Baal.[21] In fact, many of the Old Testament prophets were rewarded with social isolation because they confronted the evil and corruption of their world.

So it is today. The courageous person willing to resist corruption when one's compatriots are heavily engaged in it will pay the price of loneliness. This is one reason why churches must very intentionally provide community for those who have turned their backs on evil.

From my perspective as a table that has witnessed countless public transactions (topside) and more corrupt secret transactions than I can count (underside), there is simply no justification for corruption. It wants to spread its evil like cancer, and then, when exposed, it wants to publicly expose as many others as possible. At the end of the day, it breeds hostility and violence among its participants and loneliness among those who refuse.[22] Everyone loses in a corrupt society.

I would be delighted if my underside never witnessed another corrupt transaction!

Moral Courage in Corrupt Societies

I suggest this calls for moral courage and the willingness to stand alone, which is particularly difficult in societies that are organized communally. Western history, influenced as it is by Christianity, has long made heroes out of courageous individuals who stand alone, like Elijah and the Old Testament prophets, for example. It has honored others who stood for justice, whether Thomas More, William Wilberforce, Martin Luther King Jr., Nelson Mandela, or many others. This motif, or concept, of the courageous moral hero is grounded not only in the famous story of Socrates, but most of all in the account of Jesus' cruel death (see Chapters Two and Twelve).

The crucifixion of Jesus has inspired some of the world's most successful businesspeople, including the true story of someone who has dined at my table and who is a very successful investor. He began his professional life as a salesperson for a European company in an Asian country. In the very beginning of his now-illustrious career, his very first sale of a piece of coveted technology depended, so it seemed, upon paying a kickback to the prospective purchaser. Having grown up in a society notorious for corruption, he knew very well the "rules" for successful business. But, he was (and still is) a follower of the sinless Jesus Christ who taught His followers that neither success nor a sale justified corruption. "Be holy, because I am holy" summarized Jesus' message of moral purity 2000 years ago (in the words of one of his earliest followers).[23]

The salesman returned that evening to his hotel room, agonizing over the possibility of a lost sale because he would have to refuse the invitation to provide a kickback. The irony of it all—a young college graduate, having traveled many hours to make his first sale, only to be asked to violate his conscience by paying a kickback—made for a painful 24 hours. Nevertheless, he returned the next day, at the invitation of the prospective buyer.

"I'll buy it as it is," were the words. The implicit message: No kickback expected. Moral courage was vindicated at the very moment of greatest temptation.

In spite of some notorious failures amongst Christian leaders, true stories like this circulate in the Christian community and thus inspire similar acts of moral courage and resistance to the culture of corruption.

How do human beings resist the enormous temptation to justify corruption? Reject the idea that someone else is responsible. Each human being chooses to engage in corrupt acts, and for those they must hold us accountable. "So then, each of us will give an account of ourselves to God."[24] The corollary to this assertion is that society must hold people accountable for corrupt acts. Leaders must not be allowed to freely engage in corruption with no fear of punishment (see Chapter Eight). When humans are each personally accountable to God, then moral courage is rewarded.

Remember, while humans can blame governing authorities for failing to prosecute the corrupt, they cannot cause them to act corruptly. Romans 13 tells them to give what they owe, not what they don't. [25] Humans don't *owe* bribes to governing authorities. Instead, the Bible makes clear that humans must give to God what they owe Him, and what they owe Him is complete obedience.[26] Since He repeatedly forbids bribery and corrupt acts, what humans owe Him is clear.

Leaders who justify corruption need to change their thinking and that of their followers. They must persuade their supporters that giving them jobs for which they are not qualified is dishonest and economically disastrous. They must also make a strong case against those who argue that cultural norms demand the re-distribution of public funds to the relatives and friends of winners.

Wise leaders will, however, reason with supporters and family members. They should explain that this cultural norm undercuts human flourishing because it depends upon extracting value rather than adding value. The only way that whole economies and individual people leave poverty and thrive is by adding value and wealth, rather than extracting value, or wealth, from those who already have it. Any other idea about how economies grow is a lie that is fostered by the devil (who, as we saw in the Genesis 3 passage, is a master at deceiving nations and ethnic groups).[27] Leaders must exercise moral courage and utilize their positions to openly challenge lies that keep their people in subjection and poverty, and in turn replace these lies with economic practices (for example, capitalism and free trade) that are built on truth.[28] Rather than collecting bribes and enriching themselves, their supporters, and members of their ethnic group, leaders must take the lead in exposing evil lies that keep their people in subjection and poverty.

Finally, every human must embrace the firm and full

forgiveness that God offers to those who repent of sin (fully acknowledge their sinfulness while also seeking to turn away from sin). Judas Iscariot betrayed Jesus in a terrible way, but even he was not beyond the forgiveness of Jesus. Later he felt deep remorse, returned the money, and then killed himself. How will the corrupt of our age find redemption? Must it be at the end of a rope or the end of a leap off a bridge? No, Jesus died so that humans might be fully forgiven, even as they must justly pay restitution to those from whom they have demanded bribes.[29]

This takes moral courage, of which my underside—or my topside—has seen far too little in my many years of service.

SUMMARY

1. Humans justify corruption by:
   a. Requiring everyone to participate.
      i. When corruption is first mentioned in the Bible (Genesis 6), it was already a universal phenomenon resisted by only righteous man and his family (Noah).
      ii. Jewish leaders enlisted everyone in the plan to crucify Jesus.
      iii. Human beings exert major pressure to enlist everyone in vice, including corruption (Romans 1:18-32).
      iv. This calls for moral courage, which Jesus Christ though His Spirit has provided His followers throughout history.
   b. Spreading the blame around by making as many people as possible responsible.
   c. Expecting that politicians will reward supporters and family.
2. The social costs of corruption:
   a. Hostility and violence for those who participate
   b. Loneliness for those who don't
3. The need: Moral courage in corrupt societies, especially by leaders who ought to set the moral standard for the societies they lead

STUDY GUIDE

1. Why are people so eager to enroll everyone in the system of corruption, whether giving or taking bribes, cheating or being cheated, etc.?
2. How should the person who refuses to engage in corruption deal with others' suspicions and rejection? Consider the examples of Noah and the prophet Elijah.
3. How should leaders respond when their followers and family and ethnic group member?

NOTES

1. Richard L. Langston, *Bribery and the Bible* (Singapore: Campus Crusade Asia Limited, 1991), 29.

2. Genesis 3:6. *So when the woman saw that the tree was good for food, and that it was a delight to the eyes, and that the tree was to be desired to make one wise, she took of its fruit and ate, and she also gave some to her husband who was with her, and he ate.*

3. Genesis 6:13. *And God said to Noah, "I have determined to make an end of all flesh, for the earth is filled with violence through them. Behold, I will destroy them with the earth.*

4. Genesis 1:26. *Then God said, "Let us make man in our image, after our likeness. And let them have dominion over the fish of the sea and over the birds of the heavens and over the livestock and over all the earth and over every creeping thing that creeps on the earth."*

5. Genesis 6:9. *These are the generations of Noah. Noah was a righteous man, blameless in his generation. Noah walked with God.* Note, however, that after the Flood, Noah made some terrible errors of judgment, namely, under the effect of wine (Genesis 9:20-27).
6. Matthew 27:20. *Now the chief priests and the elders persuaded the crowd to ask for Barabbas and destroy Jesus.*

7. Matthew 26:14-16. *Then one of the twelve, whose name was Judas Iscariot, went to the chief priests and said, "What will you give me if I deliver*

him over to you?" And they paid him thirty pieces of silver. And from that moment he sought an opportunity to betray him.

8. Romans 1:29-31. *They were filled with all manner of unrighteousness, evil, covetousness, malice…envy, murder, strife, deceit, maliciousness….gossips, slanderers, haters of God, insolent, haughty, boastful, inventors of evil, disobedient to parents, foolish, faithless, heartless, ruthless.*

9. Romans 1:32. *Though they know God's righteous decree that those who practice such things deserve to die, they not only do them but give approval to those who practice them.*

10. This is a way of interpreting the sudden recognition by Adam and Eve of their nakedness (Genesis 3:7. *Then the eyes of both were opened, and they knew that they were naked. And they sewed fig leaves together and made themselves loincloths.*)

11. Genesis 3:11-13. *He said, "Who told you that you were naked? Have you eaten of the tree of which I commanded you not to eat?" The man said, "The woman whom you gave to be with me, she gave me fruit of the tree, and I ate." Then the LORD God said to the woman, "What is this that you have done?" The woman said, "The serpent deceived me, and I ate."*

12. Stephen Ellis and Gerrie Ter Haar, *Worlds of Power: Religious Thought and Political Practice in Africa* (New York: Oxford University Press, 2004), 159.

13. Genesis 2:9,16. *And out of the ground the LORD God made to spring up every tree that is pleasant to the sight and good for food. The tree of life was in the midst of the garden, and the tree of the knowledge of good and evil….And the LORD God commanded the man, saying, "You may surely eat of every tree of the garden…"*

14. Genesis 1:26. *Then God said, "Let us make man in our image, after our likeness. And let them have dominion over the fish of the sea and over the birds of the heavens and over the livestock and over all the earth and over every creeping thing that creeps on the earth."*

15. Genesis 2:24- 25. *Therefore a man shall leave his father and his mother and hold fast to his wife, and they shall become one flesh. And the man and his wife were both naked and were not ashamed.*

16. Genesis 3:15. *I will put enmity between you and the woman, and between your offspring and her offspring; he shall bruise your head, and you shall bruise his heel."*

17. Genesis 3:16. *"I will surely multiply your pain in childbearing; in pain you shall bring forth children. Your desire shall be for your husband, and he shall rule over you."*

18. Genesis 3:17-19. *And to Adam he said, "Because you have listened to the voice of your wife and have eaten of the tree of which I commanded you, 'You shall not eat of it,' cursed is the ground because of you; in pain you shall eat of it all the days of your life; thorns and thistles it shall bring forth for you; and you shall eat the plants of the field. By the sweat of your face you shall eat bread, till you return to the ground, for out of it you were taken; for you are dust, and to dust you shall return."*

19. Genesis 6:11-13. *Now the earth was corrupt in God's sight, and the earth was filled with violence. And God saw the earth, and behold, it was corrupt, for all flesh had corrupted their way on the earth. And God said to Noah, "I have determined to make an end of all flesh, for the earth is filled with violence through them. Behold, I will destroy them with the earth.*

20. I Kings 17:1-6. *Now Elijah the Tishbite, of Tishbe in Gilead, said to Ahab, "As the LORD, the God of Israel, lives, before whom I stand, there shall be neither dew nor rain these years, except by my word." And the word of the LORD came to him: "Depart from here and turn eastward and hide yourself by the brook Cherith, which is east of the Jordan. You shall drink from the brook, and I have commanded the ravens to feed you there." So he went and did according to the word of the LORD. He went and lived by the brook Cherith that is east of the Jordan. And the ravens brought him bread and meat in the morning, and bread and meat in the evening, and he drank from the brook. And after a while the brook dried up, because there was no rain in the land.*

21. I Kings 19:1-8. *Ahab told Jezebel all that Elijah had done, and how he had killed all the prophets with the sword. Then Jezebel sent a messenger to Elijah, saying, "So may the gods do to me and more also, if I do not make your life as the life of one of them by this time tomorrow." Then he was afraid, and he arose and ran for his life and came to Beersheba, which belongs to Judah, and left his servant there.*

But he himself went a day's journey into the wilderness and came and sat down under a broom tree. And he asked that he might die, saying, "It is enough; now, O LORD, take away my life, for I am no better than my fathers." And he lay down and slept under a broom tree. And behold, an angel touched him and said to him, "Arise and eat." And he looked, and behold, there was at his head a cake baked on hot stones and a jar of water. And he ate and drank and lay down again. And the angel of the LORD came again a second time and touched him and said, "Arise and eat, for the journey is too great for you." And he arose and ate and drank, and went in the strength of that food forty days and forty nights to Horeb, the mount of God.

22. Lamentations 4:3. *Even jackals offer the breast; they nurse their young, but the daughter of my people has become cruel, like the ostriches in the wilderness.*

23. I Peter 1:16. *It is written, "You shall be holy, for I am holy."*

24. Romans 14:12. *So then each of us will give an account of himself to God.*

25. Romans 13:7. *Pay to all what is owed to them: taxes to whom taxes are owed, revenue to whom revenue is owed, respect to whom respect is owed, honor to whom honor is owed.*

26. Matthew 22:21. *They said, "Caesar's." Then he said to them, "Therefore render to Caesar the things that are Caesar's, and to God the things that are God's."*

27. Revelation 12:9. *And the great dragon was thrown down, that ancient serpent, who is called the devil and Satan, the deceiver of the whole world—he was thrown down to the earth, and his angels were thrown down with him.* Revelation 20:8. *And (he) will come out to deceive the nations that are at*

the four corners of the earth, Gog and Magog, to gather them for battle; their number is like the sand of the sea.

28. The Bible also makes clear that, provided it is done without coercion, people may give wealth in order to relieve human suffering or to advance some worthy social objective. Deuteronomy 15:10. *You shall give to him freely, and your heart shall not be grudging when you give to him, because for this the LORD your God will bless you in all your work and in all that you undertake.*

29. Matthew 26:14. *Then one of the twelve, whose name was Judas Iscariot, went to the chief priests and said, "What will you give me if I deliver him over to you?" And they paid him thirty pieces of silver.*

CHAPTER FOUR

The Chair outside the Minister's Office

"Why do public employees demand bribes in order to do their duties?"

The Chair outside the Minister's Office

The corrupt often imagine that their evil behavior goes on behind closed doors without witnesses. Little do they realize that, if they could talk, there are many witnesses to the evil of corruption: plants, desks, pictures on the wall, rodents hiding in darkness, bookshelves, and, yes, chairs.

We (my colleague and I) chose a particular chair to interview. We wanted one that sat in the waiting room outside of a government minister's office, where thousands of people have occupied it during their long, tiresome waits for licenses, permissions, and favors.

People feel powerless when made to wait for endless hours, days, or weeks for government officials who love to lord it over them. These government ministers have a long history, at least as far back as the era when Jesus Christ walked this earth.[1] They conveniently forget that the term "minister" means "servant" in the Greek language from which the terms were derived. Instead, they expect others to serve them with suitably large bribes. Since many folks simply can't afford large bribes, they must wait endlessly in tired chairs like this one that dot the offices of government officials the world over.

Since so many people suffer when bribes are demanded by government employees, we wanted to hear the chair's thoughts about why public employees demand bribes in order to do their duties. Those thoughts, by way of a recorded interview, fill this chapter about government-fostered corruption.

Prepare to be astounded by the insights, biblical and otherwise, of this very experienced chair!

****

Good morning. How are you this quiet Sunday morning when most of the government offices are closed?

Relieved. It has been another long week. Some people sit on me for eight or nine hours at a time… Talk about aching backs, theirs and mine.

As a chair in the waiting room outside the office of the government's Ministry of Business, I thought you could help us understand why government officials so often demand bribes before they will undertake their public duties.

Oh my, this will be a long, long conversation. Are you sure you want to get into this?

Absolutely. My colleague and I believe that you have better insights than most, because you have been in service for so long. You have had time to both observe just about every dimension of the problem, while also having plenty of time to think about it from a biblical perspective.

Well, to understand why bribery is so central to the function of government officials, we have to do two things. First, we need to be clear there are two types of bribes: *variance* and *transactional.* A variance bribe is a bribe that enables you to bypass proper procedures, rules, and laws so that you receive what you would not ordinarily receive if justice were the norm. To illustrate it simply, if you are charged with a crime of which you are guilty, and you pay a judge to let you go free, that is a variance bribe. The Bible clearly rules variance bribes out of order.

The other kind of bribe is called a transactional bribe because, on its face, it doesn't violate the rules of justice, but does help one achieve greater speed and efficiency. If a customs officer wants a bribe to clear your shipment sitting at customs, he is probably asking for a transactional bribe. The Bible is less clear about the morality of transactional bribes, but, as I will suggest, the underlying rationale for bribes goes back to something much deeper and darker in human society. Thus, even a transactional bribe subtly interferes with justice.[2]

The first thing you need to know about government officials' demands for bribes is that there are two types. The second thing you have to realize, when thinking about government officials and bribes, is the profound influence of spirits (or, spiritual beings) on communities around the world for thousands of years. Most of the human beings in my society believe (or their grandparents or parents believed) that the physical world—rocks, hills, trees, rivers, and other features of the physical world—is animated, or made alive by spirits that cannot be seen. And they believe these spirits have the capacity to bless or to harm.[3]

Now, the key to understanding them is that they require payment before they will serve those who employ them. So, if you want to have success with your crops, then you spend a lot of money to employ a witch doctor (or shaman) to make sure the spirit whom he contacts will produce a favorable outcome for you and/or a miserable outcome for your successful neighbor. You most likely believe that there is only a fixed amount of wealth in the world, and, if he has more than you, then one way you can get some of it is to ruin his successes while simultaneously giving you successes and wealth.

These payments to the sprits are exchanges, or transactions just like you would make when you pay a shopkeeper for some bread and meat.[4]

But, how does this connect to the bribes that our government officials keep demanding?

Well, I was just coming to that. Several scholars have written that "gods can be manipulated through interpersonal moral techniques such as praise, supplication and gift giving—just as high status humans can be."[5]

Those are big words, but they are saying that giving bribes to government officials is very much like making offerings to spirits in order to motivate them to do your will. When you pay them, they do what you ask; otherwise, they don't.

Do you see why some government officials are corrupt? In what we call the pre-modern world, your ancestors bribed the spirits who were the most powerful agents for solving people's problems. In our modern era, government officials are the most powerful agents for solving problems, and so they also deserve— and expect—to be bribed. Officials become accustomed to expecting bribes, and people naturally expect to offer them, as they did (and many, many still do) to the spirits and other powers in the spirit world.

You have been thinking very hard about this, haven't you?

When your business is accommodating humans' needs to rest their tired bodies in a comfortable chair, you have a lot of time to ponder why things are the way they are.

Just as many spirits pretend to have more power than they actually do, many government officials are less powerful than they would like you to believe. Many of them are also forced to pay bribes to their bosses, and so on up the line to the very top officials. So, the pattern of powerlessness (see Chapter Two) is more prevalent and harmful than most of us realized.

Nevertheless, the first reason that public employees must be bribed is because of a reality that I call the *spirit world-government complex*. For years, as a chair I have observed what happens when citizens meet with government officials. There are three connected phenomena that reinforce each other and lead to this *complex*: 1) People believe that spirits need to be bribed in order to bring desirable results; 2) People believe that, because leaders have the capacity to manipulate the spirit world, then those leaders must be bribed; and 3) The leaders then begin to believe that they are their citizens' masters, not their servants, and thus expect to be bribed!

By contrast, in the Western countries, especially those with a heritage of Protestant Christians, government officials generally do their job without demanding an extra gratuity. They are public servants. When you are a genuine servant to the people, you serve them willingly, rather than expecting them to pay you first. Masters expect others to serve them.[6] Bribes are just one among many ways that people expect to serve government officials.

How radically unlike Jesus Christ, who said that He came not to be served, but to serve and to give His life as a ransom for many."[7] Here was One whom many thought to be the long-sought Jewish Messiah and who would lead them to victory over their hated Roman masters. Not only did He preach servant leadership; He also practiced it when he washed the feet of His closest followers.[8]

The second reason that government officials demand bribes is a problem that affects lower level government employees around the world: Their salaries are withheld by their superiors for long periods of time. In order to survive, lower level officials feel they must ask for bribes in order to undertake their public duties. Bribes are, thus, payments in lieu of government salaries. Some people justify paying these bribes in order to foster social solidarity with low-level government officials who suffer under the same tyranny of official corruption as common people.

When higher-level officials fail to pay the salaries of lower-level workers they are storing up for themselves the wrath of God: "Look! The wages you failed to pay the workers who mowed your fields are crying out against you. The cries of the harvesters have reached the ears of the Lord Almighty."[9]

The third and final reason for official corruption is buried inside each human being: You are each personally corrupt, that is, sinners who seek your selfish pleasures at the expense of God and others.[10]

I am so glad that no one is in the office today! If they had any idea about what I know about them, they would throw me out and burn me.

When you tell the truth, you make both friends and enemies, don't you? Earlier you said that spirits only do the will of those who pay them via witchdoctors, or shamans. In the same way, government officials who see themselves as lords will only do your will if you pay them.

Oh, yes, yes, yes! Many government officials are lords and masters, so that serving the people without payment is simply foreign to them. And this makes citizens angry.

But, there is another side to this: Citizens want their officials to be strong enough to magically solve their problems, just like the spirits. Citizens *want* to fear and respect their government officials as they do the spirits, with the expectation that bribes will get desirable results! Many citizens believe their leaders get their powers from the spirit world, and so a bribe may not only solicit the power of the government official but their friendly spirit as well:

> Although people are well aware of the material reasons for many of their difficulties, many also think about problems from AIDS to food shortages to corruption as having their deepest explanation in the actions of powerful figures who manipulate the spirit world.[11]

Professor Noonan at the University of California-Berkeley was one of the first to identify the connection between the practice of bribery and "witchcraft." He sees these similarities: 1) Both are usually done in secret; 2) They are socially disapproved ways of getting what you want;[12] 3) They affect the structure of society; and

4) Those bribed feel obligated, and those subject to the witch's power are tormented.[13]

Philanthropist Howard Ahmanson had in mind the *spirit world-government complex* when he recently noted that Africans vote for presidents whom they believe possess messianic powers to save citizens from governmental bureaucracies that demand bribes. In other words, they want them to have spiritual powers to protect them from what spirits (not the God of the universe) do, which is to demand bribes in order to help or to hurt. He also cleverly observed that Americans also have similar contradictory expectations of their government bureaucracies: They want bureaucrats to have near-miraculous powers to solve citizens' problems, when, in reality, government employees are mere sinful humans who also struggle to measure up to citizen expectations.

There is yet a second irony in the *spirit world-government complex*: Government officials often claim to have massive power, but by letting themselves be bribed they actually reveal how truly weak they are! The message is that their power is so limited that it is up for sale, somewhat like a prostitute's. She prances along the street to attract buyers, but in reality, she is owned by a pimp who controls and uses her to make himself rich. By analogy, government officials who demand bribes in order to perform government services are more like prostitutes.

We had no idea that the way humans relate to the spirit world has everything to do with the way they relate to government officials. So, what has to happen in order to break this spirit world-government complex?

Since the problem is spiritual, it has to be resolved spiritually.[14] There are several steps. First, you have to restore the proper relationship between the spirit world and human beings. Instead of humans sacrificing wealth in order to make the spirits do their bidding, humans have to realize that good spirits (*angels*) exist to minister to, or to serve, human beings, according to the Bible.[15] By contrast, the evil spirits (*demons*) expect you to serve them, which you ought not to do! As long as humans keep giving them offerings (with the help of witch doctors or shamans), the demons will become stronger and thus reinforce their master's (Satan) goal of deceiving the human race.

Before you go on about how to break the tight web of relationships between government officials and the spirit world, I have a very practical question: Are there any situations where bribery is justified?

In my very lowly role as a chair in government minister's waiting room, I've seen more than my share of bribes. Sometime, I would love to hear the secretary who sits in this waiting room answer the phone, "Welcome to bribe central!"

My short answer is the same one that was given by a writer in Southeast Asia: "In some extremely rare situations a bribe might be justified in stopping a grave injustice, such as an unjust execution of an innocent person by a corrupt regime, when all other possible avenues have been exhausted."[16] In general, stay away from paying bribes, not because paying a bribe is itself sinful, but because paying bribes sustains the *system* of bribery. The *system* will die if it is not fed!

Now, why do I think there may be extremely rare situations for paying bribes? They are never justified for your pleasure, ease, or access, but they may be justified to save a person's life. I can also imagine situations where government officials have not been paid for months, and their families are starving. Recast a bribe as a gift for their families, but only after carefully examining your motives to ensure that you humans are showing love to them and their innocent families, not simply trying to buy access at a border crossing, for example.

Which brings me back to the question: What does it take to break the tight connection between officials and the spirit world, what I call the *spirit world-government complex?*

For their part, citizens must first stop treating government officials as purveyors of goods and services whose powers rival those of the spirits. Government officials deserve respect, but not the adulation that is God's alone. Secondly, government officials must repent of the idea that they are lords, and begin to work instead as servants. Rather than accumulating power, their purpose is to give it away. Their call is to serve and equip citizens so that citizens will have the tools to succeed in protecting God's creation and producing what humans need in order to flourish on earth. [17]

Shortly after he was declared Israel's king, "David knew that it was the Lord who had established him as king over Israel, and that he had exalted his kingdom for the sake of his people Israel and for his [God's] own glory."[18] Being a king was not meant to exalt him personally; rather, his purpose was to exalt the whole nation so that every citizen would thrive and the other nations would come to learn about this Great God and his mercies toward all.[19]

I am amazed how you human beings miss this obvious element of leadership. What did David do when he and some of his men successfully defeated the enemy of the Amalekites? He shared the plunder with not only those who fought, but also those who didn't![20] And consider the example of Jesus: "For you know the grace of our Lord Jesus Christ, that though he was rich, yet for your sakes he became poor, so that you through his poverty might become rich."[21]

The question I have addressed is this: How should humans break the monstrous stranglehold of the *spirit world-government complex?* Citizens have to stop treating government officials like powerful spirits, and government officials need to stop treating citizens like their servants.

Those government officials who may be worshipping at this very hour must repent of the *spirit world-government* complex that has served their interests. When they renounce the spirit world and embrace Jesus Christ as Lord, they will discover that leadership means emulating Jesus' willing sacrifice so that others may live and thrive. When he spoke of the true path to leadership, Jesus said, "Whoever wants to become great among you must be your servant, and whoever wants to be first must be your slave."[22]

Meanwhile, the average citizen needs to repent of this false idea that officials are like spirits that can be bribed. That's evil and false!

This is a powerful point. I never thought about the close connection between the spirit world and bribing officials. It means a whole new way of thinking about leadership!

The following story is told among some Asian friends. A

chicken and a pig converse together in the farmyard, recounting to one another the tragic reality that 20% of the human beings are in desperate poverty. They spend almost every waking hour searching for their next meal. So, out of compassion, the chicken says, "I will lay an egg to feed the hungry." *(The other chickens in the farmyard cheer for their compassionate compatriot.)* Then the pig says, "I will become the ham to feed the hungry." *(Absolute silence descends upon the farmyard as chickens and pigs alike ponder the pig's willingness to sacrifice his life for poor human beings.)* From that story we can conclude that the willingness to personally sacrifice speaks loudly to those who follow a leader.

Besides looking out for the interests of others, rather than his own,[23] the leader who rejects corruption chooses wisdom over wealth. David's son Solomon, as he prepared to take over the monarchy, asked God for wisdom, not wealth. But, God assured him that, because his priorities were correct, God would also bless him with wealth.[24]

It's a tragedy that most of the leaders I have seen come through this office fail to model themselves after King David and his son Solomon, let alone Jesus Christ.

With your long and vast experience providing comfortable seating for those poor citizens who must wait for those officials who refuse to provide government services unless a bribe passes hands, what gives you the most hope for the future?

In the long run, my hope is that voters will elect leaders who have a demonstrated track record of resisting the lure of corruption. My greatest hope is that leaders will humble themselves under God as servants to their people, not as their masters.

SUMMARY

1. Bribes exist in two forms:
   a. Variance bribes, where a bribe is used to openly contravene the requirements of justice by causing an official to make a judgment at variance with the law.

70

      b.   Transactional bribes, where a bribe is used to speed up or make more efficient a transaction.

2.   There are three reasons government officials so often demand bribes:

      a.   The *spirit world-government complex*, which, when it occurs, is composed of three connected realities:

           i.   People believe that spirits need to be bribed in order to bring desirable results.

           ii.   People believe that, because leaders have the capacity to manipulate the spirit world, then those leaders must be bribed.

           iii.   Government officials then begin to believe that they are their citizens' masters, not their servants, and thus expect to be bribed.

      b.   Governments fail to promptly pay adequate salaries to lower-level employees, and thus force them to demand bribes in order to survive.

      c.   The sinful corruption within each human being depletes moral courage and enhances the desire for vice.

3.   The *spirit world-government complex* leads to dual ironies:

      a.   Citizens, who dislike corruption, desire corrupt leaders.

      b.   Government officials, who claim great powers for themselves, actually demonstrate their weakness by taking bribes.

4.   In order to break the power of the *spirit world-government complex:*

      a.   Citizens must stop treating officials as overly powerful.

      b.   Leaders must become servant leaders rather than masters, modeling their leadership after that of Jesus Christ.

5.   Bribes are rarely justified, except when absolutely necessary to save another's life.

The Chair outside the Minister's Office

STUDY GUIDE

1. What are the three reasons for the pervasiveness of government-fostered corruption?
2. Talk about how the spirit world-government complex impacts government-fostered corruption in your society.
3. What biblical passage helps you to see this topic in a new way?
4. How does the story of the chicken and the pig (at the very end of the chapter) motivate you to see leadership in a new light? How would you use this story with government officials that you know? How would you use the scripture to make this point with a government official who is responsive to biblical teaching?
5. What practical idea for "Taming the Beast" (found in the Appendix) will you and your group deploy as a result of reading this chapter?

NOTES

1. Mark 10:42. *And Jesus called them to him and said to them, "You know that those who are considered rulers of the Gentiles lord it over them, and their great ones exercise authority over them.*

2. cf. Richard Langston, *Bribery and the Bible* (Singapore: Campus Crusade Asia Limited, 1991), ch. 4. For a discussion of the injustice implicit in transactional bribes, see p. 63.

3. It is true that there is a lot of diversity amongst those who believe in spirits, especially when it comes to the function of mediators between humans and the spirit world. They go by different labels: shamans, witch doctors, medium, or sorcerer. However, the fundamental ideas behind what is usually called *animism* (or, *spiritism*) remain the same throughout the world, namely, that the visible material world is animated by spirit beings who require payments in order to effect the human world.

4. Stephen Ellis & Gerrie Ter Haar, *Worlds of Power: Religious Thought and Political Practice in Africa* (London: Oxford University Press, 2004), 124ff.

5. R. I. Levy, J.M. Magee & A. Howard, "Gods, spirits, and history: A theoretical perspective," in *Spirits in culture, history, and mind,* ed. J.M. Magee & A. Howard (New York: Routledge, 1996), 15.

6. Matthew 20:25. *But Jesus called them to him and said, "You know that the rulers of the Gentiles lord it over them, and their great ones exercise authority over them.*

7. Mark 10:45. *For even the Son of Man came not to be served but to serve, and to give his life as a ransom for many."*

8. John 13:1-16. *Now before the Feast of the Passover, when Jesus knew that his hour had come to depart out of this world to the Father, having loved his own who were in the world, he loved them to the end. During supper, when the devil had already put it into the heart of Judas Iscariot, Simon's son, to betray him, Jesus, knowing that the Father had given all things into his hands, and that he had come from God and was going back to God, rose from supper. He laid aside his outer garments, and taking a towel, tied it around his waist. Then he poured water into a basin and began to wash the disciples' feet and to wipe them with the towel that was wrapped around him. He came to Simon Peter, who said to him, "Lord, do you wash my feet?" Jesus answered him, "What I am doing you do not understand now, but afterward you will understand." Peter said to him, "You shall never wash my feet." Jesus answered him, "If I do not wash you, you have no share with me." Simon Peter said to him, "Lord, not my feet only but also my hands and my head!" Jesus said to him, "The one who has bathed does not need to wash, except for his feet, but is completely clean. And you are clean, but not every one of you." For he knew who was to betray him; that was why he said, "Not all of you are clean." When he had washed their feet and put on his outer garments and resumed his place, he said to them, "Do you understand what I have done to you? You call me Teacher and Lord, and you are right, for so I am. If I then, your Lord and Teacher, have washed your feet, you also ought to wash one another's feet. For I have given you an example, that you also should do just as*

I have done to you. Truly, truly, I say to you, a servant is not greater than his master, nor is a messenger greater than the one who sent him.

9. James 5:4. *Behold, the wages of the laborers who mowed your fields, which you kept back by fraud, are crying out against you, and the cries of the harvesters have reached the ears of the Lord of hosts.*

10. II Timothy 3:2-4. *For people will be lovers of self, lovers of money, proud, arrogant, abusive, disobedient to their parents, ungrateful, unholy, heartless, unappeasable, slanderous, without self-control, brutal, not loving good, treacherous, reckless, swollen with conceit, lovers of pleasure rather than lovers of God.*

11. Ellis & Ter Haar, 85, 92.

12. Remember that the Bible condemns witchcraft in passages like Deuteronomy 18:10-12. *There shall not be found among you anyone who burns his son or his daughter as an offering, anyone who practices divination or tells fortunes or interprets omens, or a sorcerer or a charmer or a medium or a necromancer or one who inquires of the dead, for whoever does these things is an abomination to the LORD. And because of these abominations the LORD your God is driving them out before you.* cf. Galatians 5:19-21. *Now the works of the flesh are evident: sexual immorality, impurity, sensuality, idolatry, sorcery, enmity, strife, jealousy, fits of anger, rivalries, dissensions, divisions.*

13. John T. Noonan, Jr., *Bribes* (New York: Macmillan, 1974), xviii.

14. Ephesians 6:10-20. *Finally, be strong in the Lord and in the strength of his might. Put on the whole armor of God, that you may be able to stand against the schemes of the devil. For we do not wrestle against flesh and blood, but against the rulers, against the authorities, against the cosmic powers over this present darkness, against the spiritual forces of evil in the heavenly places. Therefore take up the whole armor of God, that you may be able to withstand in the evil day, and having done all, to stand firm. Stand therefore, having fastened on the belt of truth, and having put on the breastplate of righteousness, and, as shoes for your feet, having put on the readiness given by the gospel of peace. In all circumstances take up the shield of faith, with which you can extinguish all the flaming darts of the evil one; and take the helmet of salvation, and the sword of the Spirit, which is the word of God, praying at all*

times in the Spirit, with all prayer and supplication. To that end keep alert with all perseverance, making supplication for all the saints, and also for me, that words may be given to me in opening my mouth boldly to proclaim the mystery of the gospel, for which I am an ambassador in chains, that I may declare it boldly, as I ought to speak.

15. Hebrews 1:14. *Are they not all ministering spirits sent out to serve for the sake of those who are to inherit salvation?*

16. Langston, 63.

17. See Chapter Twelve. cf. Robert Osburn & Ksenafo Akulli, "Does Christianity aggregate or distribute power? A historical and analytical assessment of Christianity as a power distribution mechanism," *Kairos: Evangelical Journal of Theology*, 7 (4), 183-192.

18. II Samuel 5:12. *And David knew that the LORD had established him king over Israel, and that he had exalted his kingdom for the sake of his people Israel.*

19. cf. Revelation 21:24. *By its light will the nations walk, and the kings of the earth will bring their glory into it.*

20. I Samuel 30: 22-25. *Then all the wicked and worthless fellows among the men who had gone with David said, "Because they did not go with us, we will not give them any of the spoil that we have recovered, except that each man may lead away his wife and children, and depart." But David said, "You shall not do so, my brothers, with what the LORD has given us. He has preserved us and given into our hand the band that came against us. Who would listen to you in this matter? For as his share is who goes down into the battle, so shall his share be who stays by the baggage. They shall share alike." And he made it a statute and a rule for Israel from that day forward to this day.*

21. II Corinthians 8:9. *For you know the grace of our Lord Jesus Christ, that though he was rich, yet for your sake he became poor, so that you by his poverty might become rich.*

22. Matthew 20:26-27. *It shall not be so among you. But whoever would be great among you must be your servant, and whoever would be first among you must be your slave.*

23. Philippians 2:4. *Let each of you look not only to his own interests, but also to the interests of others.*

24. I Kings 3:9ff. *Give your servant therefore an understanding mind to govern your people, that I may discern between good and evil, for who is able to govern this your great people?"*

CHAPTER FIVE

Stories from the Bank Vault

"How do modern institutions contribute to corruption?"

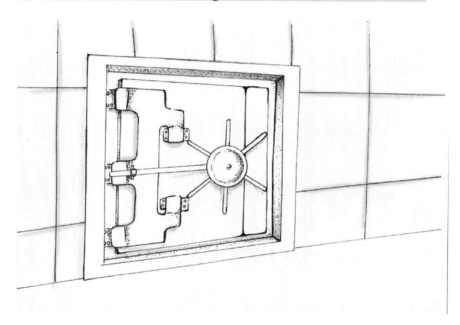

Bank vaults are peculiar places with often-colorful histories: Peculiar because no one can imagine living inside one, but colorful because their contents make them very appealing.

Especially for bank robbers. Banks have constantly innovated to stay ahead of robbers who keep devising cleverer ways to steal their valuable contents. Robbers and some government officials have much in common: No matter how sophisticated our laws and defenses, those who want to gain privately at public expense are always thinking of new, fresh ways to claim what belongs to others.

Stories from the Bank Vault

In this tale, the bank vault tells his story via a special recording smuggled out of a bank that shall, for very good reasons, remain unnamed. What the slightly-edited recording reveals about modern institutions and corruption will make us think twice about whether human beings have advanced or gone backwards. We will discover that many of the institutions we associate with modern life actually help make corruption possible.

An even bigger surprise: Many of our modern ideas about preventing corruption actually have their roots in the ancient text of the Bible. The recording—in the bank vault's distinctively tinny voice—will reveal some of the most remarkable Old Testament practices and prohibitions that guard against corruption.

****

I am humbled that you as a professor want to hear my story as a bank vault.

Thieves humble me on a regular basis. They find every ingenious way possible to steal my contents. When bank vaults were as small as safes, thieves carried them out of banks and smashed them open. Later on, thieves poured explosives through vault keyholes, blowing off the door so they could get access. When combination locks were introduced, robbers either smashed the combination lock through the door of the safe or drilled holes in the locks so they could figure out the combination. Later, robbers used cutting torches to cut holes in our sides.

Bank vaults like me have been brought to our knees time and again by those bent on robbing us. Perhaps this is how you feel when you come face to face with a government employee or a corrupt businessperson who will do anything to separate you from your money.

Having so often been outwitted by smart thieves, I wonder: Do our sophisticated laws actually deter bribery and corruption? Is it possible that our modern institutions and regulations have actually made bribery and corruption much worse than we ever imagined?

I rarely...

(A sharp metallic sound is heard on the recording, and one presumes that something awkward happened inside the vault. Did the vault flinch, thinking a robber was preparing to blow it up? Our best guess is that, for unknown reasons, a large container of valuables suddenly fell to the vault's floor. After

about 30 seconds of awkward silence, the recording resumes.)

As I was preparing to say, I rarely meet professors, at least in my world of bankers, clerks, bank regulators, and people with wealth. I hope you don't take this personally, but I've always been delightfully entertained at the thought of professors asking some of their former students for money for a building or a research program. So many of their students who earned Cs and Ds later became fabulously successful business owners (at least that happens frequently in the USA). There is a delightful little irony here: The people with the brains are asking the people with the money (their former students) for help, which is what people in the West call "role reversal!"

The folks I usually see in my vault are the bank managers and clerks who manage money and valuables for these now-wealthy, but academically-weak former students. Anyway, on a daily basis, several bank security guards enter my vault to transfer valuables into or out of me.

Now, the question that we were exploring is this: Do our modern laws and bureaucracies make corruption better or worse?

Worsening Corruption

Several professors claim their research shows that a lot of Africans believe corruption has dramatically expanded in recent years.[1] They wonder if this is because Africans are loyal to relationships, whereas Westerners (who have much, much lower rates of corruption) are loyal to law. Quite frankly, Africans have always been loyal to members of the their ethnic group. Why, then, is the problem growing?

Furthermore, the word amongst bank vaults is that corruption is growing in most of the Islamic world, Eastern Europe, and much of Latin America. (China's corruption growth rate has seemed to slow.) Is there something else besides loyalty to relationships that has, on a global basis, worsened the problem of corruption?

I suspect that the real problem might be the modern institutions, regulations, and practices that intelligent politicians and bureaucrats have created (ever since the late 1800s) for the world's nation states. Each has a whole host of institutions and laws, including a military, to protect its people. They provide a framework that has created order in global affairs, fostering successful systems and standards that facilitate global commerce and communication. As a bank vault that holds others' wealth, I gladly participate in this modern system. It ensures that money is protected, and moreover, that the banks themselves are protected by the power of the state. It also ensures that economic transactions are conducted relatively efficiently. Most people (other than bank robbers!) join me in appreciating this system.

Why Modern Institutions Can't Prevent Corruption (and May Make It Worse!)

The problem, however, is that modern systems require people to manage them, usually in some cooperative relationship between governments and private institutions like banks. The people involved will inevitably find ways to express their sinful selfishness. At customs offices, they refuse to handle paperwork from legitimate shippers and traders unless they get some money under the table. In government licensing offices, the officials and clerks find problems with paperwork until a bribe is forthcoming. When it comes to bribes for building roads, they are often at least 10% of the contract's value. Therefore, with the growth of modern institutions, there are increasingly more opportunities to serve selfish interests.

There's another problem with modern bureaucracies. They are products of the nation state. How should humans select leaders for these nation states? Most recommend democratic elections. But, the French thinker Alexis de Tocqueville warned in the 1830s that those who win democratic elections reward their supporters with gifts and favors (also known as patronage) from the public treasury. What seems like a very good system of democratic elections, especially in Western countries, often tends to reinforce corrupt behaviors.

(What follows in the next three transcribed paragraphs is a carefully and painstakingly re-constructed text. For reasons that are obvious, the content of these paragraphs is very sensitive. Apparently some authorities, when they heard about this recording, tried to digitally alter the recording at this point.

Fortunately, recording technologies are such that digital alterations are harder than most people realize, and so, with great care and attention, we were able to faithfully transcribe the somewhat scratchy recording.)

The Fox Guarding the Henhouse

I have discovered that many good modern institutions (like democratic elections) also create conditions that fuel corruption. Modern nation states promise to deliver justice for great numbers of people, so they assume great power, especially the power to tax. At the same time, they establish rules and regulations for ensuring justice in public affairs. The state hires people who function as *regulators*—to enforce these laws and to prevent corruption. The state also hires other people who conduct transactions on behalf of the state: These *managers* sign contracts for roads and other infrastructure, borrow funds from banks, and otherwise cooperate with the private sector in order to grease the wheels of the state and, ideally, the society. The regulators and managers are, in turn, both accountable to *legislators* who, supposedly, are chosen by the citizens through democratic elections to look out for their interests. Finally, the state, having hired the regulators and the managers who work for legislators, then hires a fourth category of persons called *judges*. Judges must render judgments in order to promote justice, even when those judgments involve regulators, managers, and/or legislators as defendants.

Here's the problem: The state, having taken great powers for itself in order to deliver on its grand promises to its citizens, has too many employees (regulators, facilitators, legislators, and judges) who are in its service and are beholden only to it. Only the legislators work, in part, for citizens. Why should the state's judges punish other state employees? As we say in English, "the fox guards the henhouse," which means that the state, with its massive taxing powers and monopoly over justice, protects itself and fosters the private interests of its employees in the name of the state.

So, I have concluded three things: 1) The greater the number of regulators, managers, judges, and legislators, the greater the probability of corruption; 2) When the size of projects increases, the size of bribes also increase; and 3) Those who win elections are prone to act corruptly in order to reward their supporters.

The Tragic Ejection of Christian Faith from Public Decision-Making

I have thought even more about this problem. (I have a large amount of time to think about these matters, since I must simply act big, strong, and silent in order to secure valuables from the thieves that are constantly circling.)

I already discovered that modern institutions unintentionally increase corruption because of the "fox guarding the henhouse" phenomenon, but I also discovered that these same modern institutions also rejected the one good force that could stop or slow down corruption. In the seventeenth and eighteenth centuries, thinkers concluded that justice was best achieved by ignoring biblical teaching about justice and by embracing secular non-religious principles. This historical phenomenon is called the Enlightenment.

Christianity as a religious and cultural force that could help regulate moral behavior was removed. Since the late nineteenth century, at least in Western nations, Christianity has been attacked as a collection of non-rational myths and a device to control and deceive weaker populations. Christianity's opponents claimed that science deals with reason and evidence and things that can be proven, and therefore modern systems must be built around science. Science, so they thought, would be sufficient to control the dark side of human behavior.

This assumption was a huge mistake, for many reasons. Scholars are beginning to discover that the real reason why Western, historically Protestant countries have relatively few problems with corruption is that Christianity produces people who voluntarily reject corruption and control their selfishness because of their worship of Jesus Christ[2]. Modern institutions help, but the real reason for lower rates of corruption are higher percentages of people who follow Christ.

However, when those modern institutions are exported to countries with little history of Christian moral self-restraint, then those modern systems serve the selfish, corrupt interest of those in power. I have seen the evidence: I estimate that half of the valuables stored in my vault are the fruit of corrupt practices.

When some Africans observe that premodern tribal government provided greater justice, I agree. In smaller contexts where people are somehow related and tied to each other by blood, tradition, or heritage, corruption is largely absent, first because of the lack of modern institutions that nicely serve the interests of those who extort. A second reason is because respect for ancestors ensured a code of decency, and no one, not even powerful tribal leaders, dared cross their ancestors. By contrast, absent a God of justice who truly judges all sin and injustice, modern societies have no power to rein in primordial sin and selfishness. Modern institutions have made life worse for the poor and powerless, at least in terms of corruption.

Excuse me, I must make myself available for an urgent meeting with the bank vice president....

(The recording is largely silent for about 54 minutes, except for occasional voices that sound like shouting in the background. At one point, a woman shrieks, "You have no right to tell the media! You have no right!" The voice of the bank vault initially sounds like it quivers as he begins to speak again...)

Well, it is good you didn't see what I saw. The wife of a government minister demanded that the vice president give her a huge loan on the spot, or she threatened to have his bank shut down for "illegal practices." He complied with her demand.

Modern Justifications

I am always pondering the ways that leaders justify corruption in order to make it acceptable. Friends confide in me what they hear and observe in the offices of top government officials, and one of the most common justifications is the idea that they owe something to their supporters and to their ethnic group (see Chapter Four). The leaders sound so powerless even as they strut about like powerful peacocks.

Sometimes, I wonder about you humans. Deep inside of you, there are conflicts between the moral ideals you preach and the selfishness that consumes you.

Nepotism (hiring one's relatives) is another way that corrupt leaders justify corruption. Instead of merit, blood becomes the basis for employment. God has adopted believers as His children, so we may be tempted to do likewise in the family of God. And yet, when it comes to selection criteria, the Exodus passage on the selection of judges, as well as the passage on the selection of church leaders, clearly put the emphasis on merit by virtue of performance, public-mindedness, and integrity.[3]

Wait, here comes another bank employee…

(Once again, the recording—this time it is only 13 minutes—is largely silent, except for one time when someone offered a sudden and rather ghastly gasp, as if they had stumbled upon some inexplicable evil…)

Biblical Teaching about the Proper Use of Public Funds

Before the vice president entered my vault, I was getting ready to say this: The Bible's ancient text describes practices that can dramatically reduce corruption. The first great lesson I learn from the Bible is that leaders must clearly distinguish between private and public wealth. The second is that they also must build public wealth without seeking their private benefit. Let me explain, as there are many biblical examples of these two lessons, most of them found in II Chronicles.[4]

For example, King Solomon's father David amassed precious metals not for himself but for his son to build the Jewish Temple. Instead of taking the precious metals for himself, King Solomon used them, as his father intended, to furnish the Temple, which was a public facility.[5] Later, during his reign, righteous King Asa made sure that gold and silver was stored in the Temple, rather than storing it in a private facility where he might have been tempted to steal (as happens regularly today). This was public wealth dedicated to God, and it belonged in God's House.[6]

King Jehoshaphat is another Old Testament leader who exclusively reserved public wealth for the benefit of the public, instead of his private desires. While he did accept personal gifts from the people he led,[7] when surrounding political authorities wanted to show him respect, Jehoshaphat used their donated funds to build more cities and forts, that is, public facilities.[8] How many of today's leaders would do likewise?

Another way that great leaders use great wealth to benefit the public is by building infrastructure: roads, bridges, communications facilities, and water and sewer facilities. King Uzziah used wealth to do just that,[9] as did King Jotham whose integrity contrasted with corruption amongst the larger populace.[10] But, the greatest builder of public infrastructure, as implied earlier, was David's son, King Solomon.[11] Inspired perhaps by Solomon's example, King Asa also was a great builder that benefited the Israeli public, and what is noteworthy is that his work took place during a period of great turmoil elsewhere in the Middle East.[12]

Financial transparency is another defining issue for leaders and their cronies, and is a key indicator of non-corrupt leadership. The Old Testament includes evidences of just such transparency, or visible honesty, with public finances. Under King Hezekiah a great revival broke out among the Jews, and one result was very generous giving by the people, so much so that the gifts were heaped up everywhere they could find space.[13] Hezekiah set up a transparent organization that was responsible for storing the wealth the people had donated.[14]

Public wealth, such as the valuables in the Temple, were, likewise, accounted for in a very transparent and open fashion. For example, in the period near the end of the Jews' exile to Babylon, both the Jewish leader Ezra and Darius, the non-Christian leader of the Medo-Persian Empire, made public accountings of very valuable items![15] Darius had great confidence in the Jews who had been chastened and purified by many decades of exile (597-532 BC). As a result, he entrusted funds to the Jews to rebuild their Temple, confident they would use them properly, and not for their personal benefit.[16]

Subsequently, an amazing period of religious revival broke out among the Jews who had come back from exile to the Promised Land (approximately 525 to 500 BC), and that in turn led to an explosion of trust. That trust was the foundation for an economy that started growing once again.

Here are some other examples of public transparency in the Bible:

1. Only honest contractors were to be used in building public facilities, including the Jewish temple.[17]

2. When funds were collected for the repair of the Jewish Temple, this was done in a very clear and transparent way.[18]

3. The Bible's New Testament likewise affirms the need for complete transparency. Jesus said that the secrets he told must be announced publicly, and that transparency should be the norm.[19]

What leader today (approximately 2800 to 3000 years after the Jewish kings mentioned in this chapter) is as open and honest about the use of public finances?

While it is true that the modern era has made corruption a bigger business than ever, God still reigns. Each of us, including corrupt leaders, must stand to account before Him, the Judge of the Universe. Psalms 2:10 portrays the leaders of the world at attention before God who says, "Be warned you rulers of the earth...." God holds them accountable for their massive corruption that has filled bank vaults like me to the brim. They have pocketed billions of dollars (US) without properly investing them in public infrastructure and for purposes that build their populaces.[20] Thus, "the nations have sunk in the pit that they have made; in the net that they hid, their own foot has been caught."[21] According to God, they have only one way to find peace with Him lest He judge them squarely: "Kiss the Son!"[22] *Become His obedient follower.*

And the poor who suffer because of corrupt leaders? "For the needy shall not always be forgotten, and the hope of the poor shall not perish forever."[23]

SUMMARY

1. Modern institutions and systems:
    a. Enhance commerce and communication, but are insufficient for controlling corruption.
    b. Enhance corruption, because:
        i. They provide more opportunities for human selfishness.
        ii. Democratic elections often require patronage.

       iii.   Regulators, managers, legislators, and judges are all employed by the state; hence, the "fox guards the henhouse".

    c. Rejected Christianity as a public moral force, despite new evidence that Christianity produced people who could properly control corrupt desires.

2. Common justifications for corruption today
   a. Patronage.
   b. Nepotism.

3. Biblical teaching about the administration of public finances
   a. Distinguish between private and public wealth.
   b. Use public funds for public purposes, not private interests.
   c. Transparency (visible honesty in the use of public funds).
   d. Invest in infrastructure.
   e. Remind modern leaders that they are accountable to God and that God has not forgotten the poor.

STUDY GUIDE

1. Does it surprise you that modern laws, systems, and regulations have made corruption worse, not better? Why or why not?

2. How do the examples of Israelite kings motivate you to ensure that public funds and property be used for public purposes (and not the private benefit of a government official)?

3. What changes do your regional and national leaders need to make in order to conform their practices with the Word of God?

4. What one area will you change so that your life is also conformed to His Word in this area of corruption and public finances?

5. What practical idea for "Taming the Beast" (found in the Appendix) will you and your group deploy as a result of reading this chapter?

NOTES

1. Stephen Ellis and Gerry ter Haar, *Worlds of Power: Religious Thought and Political Practice in Africa* (New York: Oxford University Press, 2004), 160.

2. E.g., Daniel Triesman, "The Causes of Corruption: A Cross-National Study," *Journal of Public Economics*, 76, 3, June 2000, 399-457.

3. Exodus 18:21. *Moreover, look for able men from all the people, men who fear God, who are trustworthy and hate a bribe, and place such men over the people as chiefs of thousands, of hundreds, of fifties, and of tens. Acts 6:3. Therefore, brothers, pick out from among you seven men of good repute, full of the Spirit and of wisdom, whom we will appoint to this duty.*

4. It is fascinating to note that II Chronicles (one of the historical books in the Bible) seems to be especially and earnestly focused on this matter of transparency by government officials. The writer of II Chronicles begins the text by recounting God's command to Solomon to live a life of righteousness and integrity. The rest of the book carries forth that expectation, even if Solomon and his successors fail. While, as a bank vault, I have no special skills as a scholar, I wonder if a scholar might want to study this theme. At any rate, one has to ask: If today's leaders refuse to repent of their corrupt ways, will God force some of them into exile so that they will learn the lessons of holiness instead of corruption?

5. II Chronicles 4: 19-22. *So Solomon made all the vessels that were in the house of God: the golden altar, the tables for the bread of the Presence, the lampstands and their lamps of pure gold to burn before the inner sanctuary, as prescribed; the flowers, the lamps, and the tongs, of purest gold; the snuffers, basins, dishes for incense, and fire pans, of pure gold, and the sockets of the temple, for the inner doors to the Most Holy Place and for the doors of the nave of the temple were of gold.*

6. II Chronicles 15:18. *And he brought into the house of God the sacred gifts of his father and his own sacred gifts, silver, and gold, and vessels.*

7. II Chronicles 17:5. *Therefore the LORD established the kingdom in his hand. And all Judah brought tribute to Jehoshaphat, and he had great riches and honor.*

8. II Chronicles 17:12. *And Jehoshaphat grew steadily greater. He built in Judah fortresses and store cities.*

9. II Chronicles 26:9-10. *Moreover, Uzziah built towers in Jerusalem at the Corner Gate and at the Valley Gate and at the Angle, and fortified them. And he built towers in the wilderness and cut out many cisterns, for he had large herds, both in the Shephelah and in the plain, and he had farmers and vinedressers in the hills and in the fertile lands, for he loved the soil.*

10. II Chronicles 27:2. *And he did what was right in the eyes of the LORD according to all that his father Uzziah had done, except he did not enter the temple of the LORD. But the people still followed corrupt practices.*

11. II Chronicles 8: 1-6. *At the end of twenty years, in which Solomon had built the house of the LORD and his own house, Solomon rebuilt the cities that Hiram had given to him, and settled the people of Israel in them. And Solomon went to Hamath-zobah and took it. He built Tadmor in the wilderness and all the store cities that he built in Hamath. He also built Upper Beth-horon and Lower Beth-horon, fortified cities with walls, gates, and bars, and Baalath, and all the store cities that Solomon had and all the cities for his chariots and the cities for his horsemen, and whatever Solomon desired to build in Jerusalem, in Lebanon, and in all the land of his dominion.*

12. II Chronicles 14: 6-7. *He built fortified cities in Judah, for the land had rest. He had no war in those years, for the LORD gave him peace. And he said to Judah, "Let us build these cities and surround them with walls and towers, gates and bars. The land is still ours, because we have sought the LORD our God. We have sought him, and he has given us peace on every side." So they built and prospered.*

13. II Chronicles 31:5-7. *As soon as the command was spread abroad, the people of Israel gave in abundance the firstfruits of grain, wine, oil, honey, and of all the produce of the field. And they brought in abundantly the tithe of everything. And the people of Israel and Judah who lived in the cities of Judah*

also brought in the tithe of cattle and sheep, and the tithe of the dedicated things that had been dedicated to the LORD their God, and laid them in heaps. In the third month they began to pile up the heaps, and finished them in the seventh month.

14. II Chronicles 31:11-19. *Then Hezekiah commanded them to prepare chambers in the house of the LORD, and they prepared them. And they faithfully brought in the contributions, the tithes, and the dedicated things. The chief officer in charge of them was Conaniah the Levite, with Shimei his brother as second, while Jehiel, Azaziah, Nahath, Asahel, Jerimoth, Jozabad, Eliel, Ismachiah, Mahath, and Benaiah were overseers assisting Conaniah and Shimei his brother, by the appointment of Hezekiah the king and Azariah the chief officer of the house of God. And Kore the son of Imnah the Levite, keeper of the east gate, was over the freewill offerings to God, to apportion the contribution reserved for the LORD and the most holy offerings. Eden, Miniamin, Jeshua, Shemaiah, Amariah, and Shecaniah were faithfully assisting him in the cities of the priests, to distribute the portions to their brothers, old and young alike, by divisions, except those enrolled by genealogy, males from three years old and upward—all who entered the house of the LORD as the duty of each day required—for their service according to their offices, by their divisions. The enrollment of the priests was according to their fathers' houses; that of the Levites from twenty years old and upward was according to their offices, by their divisions. They were enrolled with all their little children, their wives, their sons, and their daughters, the whole assembly, for they were faithful in keeping themselves holy. And for the sons of Aaron, the priests, who were in the fields of common land belonging to their cities, there were men in the several cities who were designated by name to distribute portions to every male among the priests and to everyone among the Levites who was enrolled.*

Unfortunately, according to II Chronicles 32:27-29, Hezekiah let himself get taken away with pride, and eventually did start piling up great riches for himself. Some of it was probably God's blessing upon him (v. 29) but some of it was a function of his arrogance and pride at being successful (II Chronicles 32:25).

15. Ezra 1:7-11. *Cyrus the king also brought out the vessels of the house of the LORD that Nebuchadnezzar had carried away from Jerusalem and placed in the house of his gods. Cyrus king of Persia brought these out in the*

charge of Mithredath the treasurer, who counted them out to Sheshbazzar the prince of Judah. And this was the number of them: 30 basins of gold, 1,000 basins of silver, 29 censers, 30 bowls of gold, 410 bowls of silver, and 1,000 other vessels; all the vessels of gold and of silver were 5,400. All these did Sheshbazzar bring up, when the exiles were brought up from Babylonia to Jerusalem. Ezra 2:68-69. *Some of the heads of families, when they came to the house of the LORD that is in Jerusalem, made freewill offerings for the house of God, to erect it on its site. According to their ability they gave to the treasury of the work 61,000 darics of gold, 5,000 minas of silver, and 100 priests' garments.;* Ezra 8:28ff. *Guard them and keep them until you weigh them before the chief priests and the Levites and the heads of fathers' houses in Israel at Jerusalem, within the chambers of the house of the LORD."*

16. Ezra 6:4,8. *"Let the cost be paid from the royal treasury...Moreover, I make a decree regarding what you shall do for these elders of the Jews for the rebuilding of this house of God. The cost is to be paid to these men in full and without delay from the royal revenue, the tribute of the province from Beyond the River."* Ezra 7:15ff. *Carry the silver and gold that the king and his counselors have freely offered to the God of Israel, whose dwelling is in Jerusalem.*

17. II Kings 12:15. *And they did not ask for an accounting from the men into whose hand they delivered the money to pay out to the workmen, for they dealt honestly.*

18. II Chronicles 24:8. *So the king commanded, and they made a chest and set it outside the gate of the house of the LORD.* cf. II Kings 12:9-16. *Then Jehoiada the priest took a chest and bored a hole in the lid of it and set it beside the altar on the right side as one entered the house of the LORD. And the priests who guarded the threshold put in it all the money that was brought into the house of the LORD. And whenever they saw that there was much money in the chest, the king's secretary and the high priest came up and they bagged and counted the money that was found in the house of the LORD. Then they would give the money that was weighed out into the hands of the workmen who had the oversight of the house of the LORD. And they paid it out to the carpenters and the builders who worked on the house of the LORD, and to the masons and the stonecutters, as well as to buy timber and quarried stone for making repairs on the house of the LORD, and for any outlay for the*

repairs of the house. But there were not made for the house of the LORD basins of silver, snuffers, bowls, trumpets, or any vessels of gold, or of silver, from the money that was brought into the house of the LORD, for that was given to the workmen who were repairing the house of the LORD with it. And they did not ask for an accounting from the men into whose hand they delivered the money to pay out to the workmen, for they dealt honestly. The money from the guilt offerings and the money from the sin offerings was not brought into the house of the LORD; it belonged to the priests.

19. Matthew 10:27. *What I tell you in the dark, say in the light, and what you hear whispered, proclaim on the housetops.* Mark 4:11. *And he said to them, "To you has been given the secret of the kingdom of God, but for those outside everything is in parables."*

20. A major exception to this rule are the largely Western countries, especially those with an historical Protestant heritage. These are the countries that have a history of investing in public infrastructure, and, as we will see later in this book, they are also noted for very low levels of corruption. Is there a correlation between their Protestant Christian heritage, well-developed infrastructure, and low levels of corruption?

21. Psalm 9:15. *The nations have sunk in the pit that they made; in the net that they hid, their own foot has been caught.*

22. Psalm 2:12. *Kiss the Son, lest he be angry, and you perish in the way, for his wrath is quickly kindled. Blessed are all who take refuge in him.* cf. Psalm 9:20. *Let the nations know that they are but men!*

23. Psalm 9:18. *For the needy shall not always be forgotten, and the hope of the poor shall not perish forever.*

CHAPTER SIX

The Computer Terminal Tells All

"Why is greed a powerful cause of corruption?"

The Computer Terminal Tells All

As laptops and mobile devices replace them, computer terminals around the world are a slowly dying breed. But, in many countries where corruption is everywhere present, they still get an amazing workout. Often, for 24 hours each day, fingers tap out messages on their keyboards, inviting millions of unsuspecting readers around the world to help "claim" lost, forgotten, concealed, or banked funds (with the promise that the readers will get a share of the loot).

Known as 419 Letters, *these dishonest and deceptive online appeals require upfront payment of fees in order to gain access to large amounts of wealth.* 419 Letters *are one of the many dozens of "confidence tricks" meant to separate the naïve and gullible from their wealth.*

A large percentage of 419 Letters *are written in Nigerian computer cafes[1] (and, increasingly, in other nations of the world, as well). They have successfully looted millions from online and other readers that they have invited to share in the schemes. Greedy Nigerians (and others around the world) appeal to the greed of those who read their fictitious letters. (Doesn't this remind you about what we learned from the purse in Chapter Two? Our corrupt souls make us easy victims of those who appeal to our greed and corruption.)*

This tale concerns a discarded computer that we discovered in one of Lagos, Nigeria's many computer recycling centers. Having secretly signaled its desire to converse with us, we asked it why corruption is so powerfully motivated by human greed. Since this computer was powerfully programmed for communication with humans, the result is a very revealing conversation. To ensure the confidentiality of our computer informant, we will call her "Zorte."

Sadly, by the time you read this, Zorte will have met her demise. She will have been torn apart and recycled to sundry places around the world.

****

Sorry to be so late, Zorte. It took me hours to crawl five kilometers through the horrible traffic here in Lagos. Thanks so much for waiting for me.

No problem! Since I am waiting to be recycled, I have plenty of time to think about greed and corruption. Anyway, in spite of the terrible traffic, did you notice the vibrant risk-taking spirit of business people here in Lagos?

Energy and intensity. Wow. I admit that I am blown away.

That's the thing about the *419 Letters*: People look for every avenue—legal and illegal—to gain wealth. Some are trying to survive, and many are motivated by pure greed.

Although I am a mere computer, I've learned a lot about how humans function: As His image bearers, humans are created by God to be producers, and it is that production of goods and services that drives most healthy economies. What you call "the profit motive" is very alive here in Nigeria. There is something very exciting and satisfying about trying to make a *naira* (the Nigerian currency) every time you sell something. Functionally, economists call this process "value-adding." But, there is something else that motivates and drives human beings, something that comes from a very, very dark and dangerous place inside their souls. And that something is connected to a problem I call "faulty worship."

There is something going on that makes you stop and shudder sometimes...

People want more than they need, lots more, right? Greed, greed, greed. Every single day when I was in active service as a computer I felt the human impulse to greed. Research in the USA indicates that most people, whether they are rich or poor, when asked "How much money do you need to live in the way you would like to live?" will answer "20% more than I have right now."

From your perspective as a computer, my question to you is "Why?"

It's tempting to think that people are merely dissatisfied with their lives as they are. But you have to remember that there are large numbers of people in this huge metropolis (or whatever you wish to call it) who have no idea where their next bowl of food will come from. With my webcam I could see the hollow, vacant look of fear and desperation in their poverty-stricken eyes. The Bible has a remarkable passage that reads: "Give me neither poverty nor riches; feed me with the food that is needful for me, lest I be full and deny You and say, "Who is the LORD?" or lest I be poor and steal and profane the name of my God."[2] I always felt a deep sense of empathy for those haunted by desperate hunger. But, something very dark goes on inside of the human soul that explains the unending desire for "more."

So you are saying that, while some of the people who write the 419 Letters are miserably hungry, there is also something wrong spiritually, at least with those who set up these operations?

Absolutely. The people employed by the owners of the 419 operations were hungry. When it comes to greed, the people who *own* these 419 operations are the real problem. These enterprising businesspeople are greedy for more, more, more!

At the same time, I admire the honesty of most Nigerians: They actually condemn themselves as "corrupt" people, even while also actively participating in corruption. I am impressed by this honesty, but heartbroken to see that the people who used me were still so tied up with what they otherwise condemn.[3] If you read your Bible, you will discover that the Apostle Paul described this situation perfectly in Romans 7 when he wrote, "I do not do the good I want, but the evil I do not want is what I keep on doing" (v. 19). Sin has enormous power to subvert even our best motives, a fact that ought to drive every human being to their knees.

Well, let's find out why people are so greedy. Give me your thoughts, will you? You seem to know how to quote the Bible, and, as you told me earlier, your hard drive is full of Bible software. Part of me is a little skeptical: Is Christianity a convenient, but powerless faith, especially here in southwest Nigeria?

This is very interesting! Some of your suspicions are warranted, but I have seen and heard too much to consider Christianity a powerless faith. Nevertheless, as I have scanned and studied the biblical text that a godly Yoruba pastor loaded into my hard drive, I discovered that the central issue behind greed is idolatry.

This is challenging! Tell me more...

Well, start with the New Testament, and then we will work back to the Old Testament. The Apostle Paul on two occasions offers a list of sins from which Christians should abstain. In Colossians 3:5, for example, he wrote under the inspiration of God's Spirit about sins like "sexual immorality, impurity, passion and evil desire" *without* qualification or further explanation. But, then, when he lists the sin of "greed," he adds this explanation: "which is idolatry." Did you hear that?! Paul repeats this in Ephesians 5:5 because he thought most people wouldn't realize the seriousness of greed unless he called it idolatry, which was a shocking accusation in first century Jewish culture.[4] Paul is saying: Stop substituting devotion to God with devotion to something He has created or which humans have created. This is very, very serious!

This is stunning. Help me to think about what this means in practical terms.

Well, sure, but let's first make another observation along these same lines. In Exodus 20, where we read about the famed Ten Commandments, greed is likened to covetousness, that is, desiring something that doesn't belong to you.[5] So, greedy people are both idolaters and coveters. They wrongly want what others have but which they are not entitled to. In practical terms, corruption is fueled by greed that is stimulated by improper devotion to something in creation and the improper desire for others' possessions.

That to which you are devoted rules your life. You make sacrifices for it, even if it costs you something. When the Children of Israel were in the desert on their long, slow trek to the Promised Land, they made an idol in the form of a golden calf while Moses was on Mount Sinai receiving the 10 Commandments. They did this despite: 1) Moses' assurances that he was traveling to meet with God; 2) God's provision for the Jewish people (meat, bread, and water); and 3) His giant miracle in letting them escape Egypt through the Red Sea.

You are either properly devoted to God or improperly to something He created (that is called idolatry). Greed is improper devotion to wealth, and that is what powers corruption. Taming the beast called corruption is more than a Western-sponsored program to make everyone accountable to abstract rules and regulations designed to stop corruption; rather, it means aggressively converting our deepest devotion from wealth to God. Very simply, corruption is a problem of faulty worship, that is, having the wrong object of worship.

Are you still with me? Since I am a computer, I am used to being long-winded…

Yes, yes.

Faulty worship plus the improper desire for others' possessions is a very powerful fuel that powers corruption. To sum up, we worship what we shouldn't (greed) while also desiring what we shouldn't (covetousness). That powerful combination breeds a very stubborn case of corruption.

Wait a minute. Let's go back to the golden calf. When I check my Bible, it seems to say in Exodus 32 that when the people of Israel made the golden calf, they became "corrupt." Help me better understand this connection between idolatry and corruption.[6]

I have been thinking long and hard about this. It helps to have a big hard drive! First, corruption is a pervasive rot that destroys what may have once been a very fine society (see Chapter One). Good quality iron that rusts will slowly disintegrate and become worthless over time.

Idolatry rusts away the cultural core of an otherwise healthy society because you trust what is tangible and temporary, instead of the invisible God who makes healthy societies resilient and enduring when attacked from within and without.

Greed means you trust in that which can be destroyed at any time, either through thievery, fire, storms, or whatever.[7] When you think about it, greed is a very, very ignorant devotion to that which can never give human beings and their societies the resilience they need.

Idolatry is connected to corruption because idols feed a lie about what will last forever (money), thus setting us up to lose everything worth having (God). In the case of the Jewish people who were still looking for their Promised Land, their idolatry was setting them up for weakness due to cultural and social rotting, and there was no way they would have ever conquered the Canaanites and taken the Promised Land as a weak people.

Today's leaders who insist on being corrupt only weaken their societies by fostering the lie that money and goods are what endure. What they should do, instead, is set examples of proper devotion to God, because only that kind of devotion will produce the strong, enduring cultures and societies they want to lead and in which their people want to live.

The future of whole nations is at stake unless corruption is tamed and conquered!

I repeat: Greed is the destructive idol that corrupts societies, and corrupt societies become weak nations.

The logic is simple: Greed is an idol. Idols fuel corruption. Corruption slowly destroys societies from within. Leaders who participate in corruption are slowly destroying their societies.

Ever notice how corrupt dictators never seem to have enough? They always need more, more, more! I heard that the leader of one notoriously corrupt nation (where the gross domestic product per capita is little more than $700/year) is worth US$15 billion by himself. That doesn't count the wealth of all his family members and the other politicians around him. Virtually all their wealth is a product of the greed-driven phenomenon that we call corruption.

Of course, you have to go to China to see massive piles of cash, hoarded in room after room of those whose greed knows no bound! Some of them have run out of room storing all this cash in their houses, and so they are hiding the cash in all kinds of places: the bottom of lakes, inside trees, in their automobiles, and every place they can imagine![8]

When you trust in the wrong thing—that which can be destroyed by thievery, fire, or storms—you have this endless desire for more, more, more. But as my friend, the bank vault in Chapter Five, knows, even a bank vault can't provide absolute security. In the process, trust in idols disintegrates not only what faith you may have had in God, but it ultimately disintegrates your society so that it becomes weak and vulnerable to those who want to destroy it.

But so many corrupt leaders like to be seen in religious centers...

Trust me: When the corrupt show up in church, they are absolutely deceiving themselves if they imagine God does not see their wickedness. The only thing they should be doing in church is repenting of their sins, seeking God with all their hearts, returning the money to whom it belongs (usually the citizens of their countries), and setting in place systems to ensure that no one else enriches themselves at public expense.[9] If they want to have strong nations, they must do this before it is too late!

Are you tired? We computers don't really ever get tired. Overheated, yes, but never tired.

Well, it has been a long day, but you really have me pondering what you have said, Zorte. This link between greed, idolatry, and corruption has been around a long time, no doubt.

Absolutely. When financial interests are threatened by what the Gospel does in people's lives, those interests react violently. When the Apostle Paul cast the demon out of a slave girl who was a fortuneteller, her owners became enraged at Paul. They had lost what Americans call their "cash cow!"[10] And when the makers of idols in the city of Ephesus discovered that new Christians were destroying their idols, the idol makers grew furious.[11] Idolatry is big business, just as is corruption.

Let's go back to 419 Letters. Nigerians pounded the keys on your keyboard for years. How does greed fuel the corruption called the 419 Letter?

The letters assume that both senders and readers are greedy. When the Westerner (the usual recipient of such letters) opens the email letter (or text message) that claims to be from the wife of some late dictator, "she" asks the Western reader to help her hide

100

away some of her millions of US dollars. If the Western reader helps her, she promises him part of the loot, but only if the Westerner sends some funds to show that he or she is a sincere partner in helping hide the money!

As some in the West say, "It takes two to tango!"[12] And when it comes to *419 Letters*, both the sender and the receiver have to be devoted to money as their idols in order for the *419 Letters* to work. A shared devotion to greed. Simple as that!

Now, to make these *419 Letters* (which have been sent by the thousands from me at any given time) work, several factors are needed to activate greed in the heart of the Western reader. First of all, he or she has to feel like the writer (whomever that may be) is inviting her or him into their confidence. It has to feel like a "little secret just between us." Professors call this a "confidence trick." This gains the trust of the reader. The reader on the other end has to believe that your story is true before they will send you money so that you, in turn, will send them your funds for safekeeping in some Western bank.

After gaining people's trust through sharing a secret, a second aspect comes into play in *419 Letters*: Once the money is deposited in the account of the trickster who runs the *419 Letter* hoax, then all contact with the Western collaborator stops. Hopefully, the Westerner will use their sense of bitter betrayal to look inside themselves and discover that their idolatrous heart of greed needs to be conquered by Christ. If I were a Christian, I would look for those moments when people can be persuaded to abandon idols and turn to the living God.

Think about the betrayer of Jesus Christ. Judas Iscariot, one of Jesus' twelve apostles, was an insider in charge of the moneybag. In reality, he was very greedy. He asked Jesus' chief opponents, "What will you give me if I deliver him over to you?"[13] They gave him what in most people's minds was an incredible amount of money.[14] Judas was a very greedy man whose life was secretly devoted to idols, and that means corruption. Corruption rots the soul of people and of nations. Ultimately, it is a killer, and that is exactly what happened to Judas: He killed himself.

Judas' corruption came back to haunt him.[15]

Because of Judas' idolatrous greed, Jesus' life was sacrificed. Because He is God, Jesus' self-sacrifice did something completely unexpected: He undermined the power of greed over human hearts by making it possible for people to re-direct their devotion to God. Judas' corruption literally fueled the beginning of the movement that undermines it!

The Apostle Paul wrote "But those who desire to be rich fall into temptation, into a snare, into many senseless and harmful desires that plunge people into ruin and destruction."[16] Jesus' brother James wrote about greed: "Now listen, you rich people, weep and wail because of the misery that is coming upon you. Your wealth has rotted, and moths have eaten your clothes. Your gold and silver are corroded. Their corrosion will testify against you and eat your flesh like fire. You have hoarded wealth in the last days."[17]

I wish that I could deliver a message to every businessman and shady operator who sends young men and women to write *419 Letters* on my keyboard: Greed is costly to the greedy! First of all, it's costly to your reputation. People rapidly lose trust in you when they know you can be purchased. Your spouse will lose trust that you are faithful. Friends quickly scatter when they think their secrets can be sold to the highest bidder! Greed not only fuels the corruption that destroys, but greed also makes you lonely.

Secondly, greed is a cheater that lets you down. It pretends to offer security, but the wealth you accumulate through corruption communicates a false message: "You are now safe from any and every possible threat to your life." How well did his vast corrupt wealth serve Omar Gadhafi at the moment of his violent death? What about Saddam Hussein at the moment he was hung? What about some of China's top government officials whom Xi Jinping has sent to prison?

Ouch. And I suppose you would say that every corrupt official—at least those who are masters of corruption—will spend eternity in hell after they die, no matter how many churches they attended or pulpits from which they delivered their Christian testimony.

What other destiny could await those who have stolen the

wealth of so many millions? They have not only stolen what little wealth the masses have accumulated, but they have, in fact, stolen their labor. Most people have earned their small amount of wealth through labor, often hard labor, and yet these corrupt officials demand that wealth for themselves. If God violently drowns those who cause young believers to sin,[18] then I have little doubt that He has mapped out a similar destiny for corrupt officials who absolutely refuse to repent and pay back those from whom they steal.

Greed fuels corruption, and corruption finally destroys. It destroys whole societies, and it ultimately destroys humans in an eternity that, whether a hell of supreme loneliness and isolation or a hell of extreme torment and suffering, is no place for human beings.[19]

As a computer, I don't have that destiny. Someday soon I will be chopped up for parts and recycling. That's nothing like the future of the idolater and the covetous who run from God to greed and corruption.

So, is there any hope for these people?

Actually, there is. It's very simple: Turn from cleverness, greed, idolatry, covetousness, and *419 Letters*. Turn to God by placing your devotion on Jesus, the sinless One who died for you. If you read the stories in Genesis of Abraham and Sarah, and their son Isaac and grandson Jacob, you see a pattern of cleverness. But, along the way, each of those great patriarchs eventually renounced their clever plans and embraced the God who created them to enjoy a different kind of wealth.

Did you know that God explicitly instructed the Jews to desire a king *without* a greedy heart? Instead, a great king had to first desire the Word of God, revering it and following it carefully.[20] Isn't that the kind of leader we want today?

Having scanned thousands of files that have come across my screen, I have learned an important lesson: In countries that have, at least in the past, been deeply influenced by Christian teaching, most government officials and parliamentarians serve in order to contribute to their society, not to become rich. Most are already rich, and usually pursue public service with a sense of obligation and a desire to improve the society.

Likewise, I have learned that there are many successful businesses created around principles of virtue and an absolute refusal to engage in corruption. I recommend reading Theodore Malloch's *Spiritual Enterprise: Doing Virtuous Business* (2008).

Read Psalm 112, and see what it says about the man who is truly rich: He delights in God's Word; his offspring are powerful, significant folks; he is persistently righteous, gracious, merciful, and generous with the poor to whom he lends funds; he is known for justice; he is not anxious, but trusts God even when things go badly; and he is fondly remembered long after his death.

Can anyone who reads this Psalm deny that absolute honesty, kindness, justice, and generosity are the keys to wealth? Does anyone honestly believe that corruption is the path to true wealth?

You know, for a simple computer, you are quite a Bible scholar! So, let's conclude this interview with one more question: How do those in power resist corruption when they are constantly tempted by those who try to shove gifts at them?

I'm so glad you mentioned the fact that contractors, working associates, parents, and others try to give gifts—call them "grease"— to government officials and teachers.

Now, to be clear, in some societies, small gifts are a delightful way to freshen and nurture relationships. You can hardly expect people to stop giving such token gifts! But, when they start giving gifts of substance, then innocent gifts become "grease."

The official has to adopt God's attitude: I cannot and will not be bribed.[21] When the gift suddenly appears on your desk or in your hand, you politely return it and tell the giver that you cannot accept it. Never think twice; always return the gift immediately.

If you are a high government official, refusing bribes may make enemies of other high government officials. By refusing the gifts, you are no longer a member of the "team," so they say. That vicious attack can be countered by reminding them if God can't be bribed, then why should you? You can also tell them how Jewish government officials, as recorded in the Old Testament, handled funds with great honesty:

1. When the Israelites gave money for the sanctuary, Moses, the courageous leader who led the Jews from Egypt to the Promised Land, refused to skim off a portion for himself.[22,23]
2. The skilled craftsmen hired to build the sanctuary were so honest that they begged the people to <u>stop</u> bringing offerings![24]
3. King David, rather than enriching himself, took all the valuable metals that were given to him and dedicated them to God.[25] Remember that David faced temptations like all of us. He failed spectacularly when he took another man's wife and subsequently killed her husband. Later, David repented and God forgave Him.

Leaders need to be reminded daily that their corruption will silently fuel a movement, violent or otherwise, for a change in leadership. When the two sons of Eli, the chief priest around 1100 BC, became corrupt, Eli's leadership began to slip.[26] When Samuel's son slipped into a similar patter of corruption, the people had had enough.[27] They demanded a monarchy that produced both good kings (like David) and bad kings (like so many others). What people want, more than almost anything else, is a leader who "rejects gain from extortion and keeps his hand from accepting bribes."[28]

Thank you, Zorte. This has been a fascinating interview. Now I see clearly that, as you said earlier, we devote ourselves to what we can see with our eyes and we desire what we shouldn't. But, I also realize that, by re-directing our devotion to God, leaders who model themselves after leaders like Moses and David can refuse the bribes that people offer.

SUMMARY

1. The human drive to produce goods and services, itself a function of our design as God's image bearers, can be motivated by real need or by greed.
2. Greed is the destructive idol that in turn corrupts societies, and corrupt societies become weak nations.
   a. Greed makes us devote ourselves to and desire

what we shouldn't.

   b. Idolatry is fed by the false belief that what is temporary will last forever, while simultaneously disintegrating faith in the invisible, but living God.

   c. Corruption :

      i. Depends upon the motivating power of greed.

      ii. Ultimately destroys nations and make people lonely.

   d. Only Jesus the Savior can deliver us from the idolatry and covetousness that fuels our corruption.

3. Averting God's judgment for a life of corruption means:

   a. Turning to God by devoting yourself to Jesus Christ

   b. Refusing all gifts

   c. Following the example of great biblical leaders who resisted the lure of personal enrichment

4. Bribes and gifts can and should be refused by government officials and teachers.

STUDY GUIDE

1. "People who want to get rich fall into temptation and a trap and into many foolish and harmful desires that plunge men into ruin and destruction."[29] Whom do you know that has suffered this outcome due to too much wealth? Why do we imagine that if we were in his/her shoes, we would not have these consequences?

2. Read Matthew 6:19-21, 33. Where should we truly seek our wealth? Why don't we? What do these lessons about greed (in this chapter) reveal about your internal desires?

3. Why is greed an idol that ultimately fuels the corruption that weakens nations?

4. Consider this statement from our chapter: "Greed is an idol. Idols fuel corruption. Corruption slowly destroys societies from within. Leaders who participate in corruption are slowly destroying their societies." How will you communicate this message to others?

5. How can we help those betrayed (by such confidence tricks

as *419 Letters*) to transfer their devotion from money, or wealth, to Christ?

6. What practical idea for "Taming the Beast" (found in the Appendix) will you and your group deploy as a result of reading this chapter?

NOTES

1. Donald J. Smith, *A Culture of Corruption: Everyday Deception and Popular Discontent in Nigeria* (Princeton, NJ: Princeton University Press, 2008).

2. Proverbs 30:8-9. *Remove far from me falsehood and lying; give me neither poverty nor riches; feed me with the food that is needful for me, lest I be full and deny you and say, "Who is the LORD?" or lest I be poor and steal and profane the name of my God.*

3. See Smith, 2007.

4. *For you may be sure of this, that everyone who is sexually immoral or impure, or who is covetous (that is, an idolater), has no inheritance in the kingdom of Christ and God.*

5. Exodus 20:17. *You shall not covet your neighbor's house; you shall not covet your neighbor's wife, or his male servant, or his female servant, or his ox, or his donkey, or anything that is your neighbor's.*

6. Exodus 32:7-8. *And the LORD said to Moses, "Go down, for your people, whom you brought up out of the land of Egypt, have corrupted themselves. They have turned aside quickly out of the way that I commanded them. They have made for themselves a golden calf and have worshiped it and sacrificed to it and said, 'These are your gods, O Israel, who brought you up out of the land of Egypt!'" cf. Deuteronomy 4:15-16. "Therefore watch yourselves very carefully. Since you saw no form on the day that the LORD spoke to you at Horeb out of the midst of the fire, beware lest you act corruptly by making a carved image for yourselves, in the form of any figure, the likeness of male or female."*

7. Matthew 6:19-21. *Do not lay up for yourselves treasures on earth, where moth and rust destroy and where thieves break in and steal, but lay up for yourselves treasures in heaven, where neither moth nor rust destroys and where thieves do not break in and steal.*

8. The Chinese government has, at least on paper, strict laws about corruption, and so those carrying huge piles of cash to deposit in bank accounts signal bank officials to alert government authorities concerning possible incidences of corruption.

9. Deuteronomy 4:25. *"When you father children and children's children, and have grown old in the land, if you act corruptly by making a carved image in the form of anything, and by doing what is evil in the sight of the Lord your God, so as to provoke him to anger."*

10. Acts 16:16-19. *As we were going to the place of prayer, we were met by a slave girl who had a spirit of divination and brought her owners much gain by fortune-telling. She followed Paul and us, crying out, "These men are servants of the Most High God, who proclaim to you the way of salvation." And this she kept doing for many days. Paul, having become greatly annoyed, turned and said to the spirit, "I command you in the name of Jesus Christ to come out of her." And it came out that very hour.*

11. Acts 19:25. *These he gathered together, with the workmen in similar trades, and said, "Men, you know that from this business we have our wealth."*

12. The tango is a dance made famous in Buenos Aires, Argentina.

13. Matthew 26:15. *"When you father children and children's children, and have grown old in the land, if you act corruptly by making a carved image in the form of anything, and by doing what is evil in the sight of the LORD your God, so as to provoke him to anger."*

14. The value of 30 pieces of silver is hard to calculate between and among nations. One person suggested it would be like US$15,000 today, which, in many parts of the world, would be like two or three years' worth of income.

15. Matthew 27:3ff. *Then when Judas, his betrayer, saw that Jesus was condemned, he changed his mind and brought back the thirty pieces of silver to the chief priests and the elders.*

16. I Timothy 6:9. *But those who desire to be rich fall into temptation, into a snare, into many senseless and harmful desires that plunge people into ruin and destruction.*

17. James 5:1-3. *Come now, you rich, weep and howl for the miseries that are coming upon you. Your riches have rotted and your garments are moth-eaten. Your gold and silver have corroded, and their corrosion will be evidence against you and will eat your flesh like fire. You have laid up treasure in the last days.*

18. Matthew 18:6. *But whoever causes one of these little ones who believe in me to sin, it would be better for him to have a great millstone fastened around his neck and to be drowned in the depth of the sea.*

19. To be very clear, hell is the destiny of those who reject the offer of salvation and eternal life through Jesus Christ, as I will note later in this chapter. Corruption is only one of the sins for which Jesus paid the ultimate price on the Cross so that we would not only spend eternal life with him but also develop the integrity that rejects corruption (see Chapter 12).

20. I Chronicles 28:9. *"And you, Solomon my son, know the God of your father and serve him with a whole heart and with a willing mind, for the LORD searches all hearts and understands every plan and thought. If you seek him, he will be found by you, but if you forsake him, he will cast you off forever."*

21. Deuteronomy 10:17. For *the LORD your God is God of gods and Lord of lords, the great, the mighty, and the awesome God, who is not partial and takes no bribe.*

22. Exodus 36:3. *And they received from Moses all the contribution that the people of Israel had brought for doing the work on the sanctuary. They still kept bringing him freewill offerings every morning.*

23. Numbers 3:46-51. "*And as the redemption price for the 273 of the firstborn of the people of Israel, over and above the number of the male Levites, you shall take five shekels per head; you shall take them according to the shekel of the sanctuary (the shekel of twenty gerahs), and give the money to Aaron and his sons as the redemption price for those who are over.*" *So Moses took the redemption money from those who were over and above those redeemed by the Levites. From the firstborn of the people of Israel he took the money, 1,365 shekels, by the shekel of the sanctuary. And Moses gave the redemption money to Aaron and his sons, according to the word of the LORD, as the LORD commanded Moses.*

24. Exodus 36:5. *And said to Moses, "The people bring much more than enough for doing the work that the LORD has commanded us to do."*

25. II Samuel 8:11. *These also King David dedicated to the LORD, together with the silver and gold that he dedicated from all the nations he subdued.* I Chronicles 18:11. *These also King David dedicated to the LORD, together with the silver and gold that he had carried off from all the nations, from Edom, Moab, the Ammonites, the Philistines, and Amalek.*

26. I Samuel 2:22-24. *Now Eli was very old, and he kept hearing all that his sons were doing to all Israel, and how they lay with the women who were serving at the entrance to the tent of meeting. And he said to them, "Why do you do such things? For I hear of your evil dealings from all these people. No, my sons; it is no good report that I hear the people of the LORD spreading abroad."*

27. I Samuel 8: 1-5. *When Samuel became old, he made his sons judges over Israel. The name of his firstborn son was Joel, and the name of his second, Abijah; they were judges in Beersheba. Yet his sons did not walk in his ways but turned aside after gain. They took bribes and perverted justice. Then all the elders of Israel gathered together and came to Samuel at Ramah and said to him, "Behold, you are old and your sons do not walk in your ways. Now appoint for us a king to judge us like all the nations."*

28. Isaiah 33:15. *He who walks righteously and speaks uprightly, who despises the gain of oppressions, who shakes his hands, lest they hold a bribe, who stops his ears from hearing of bloodshed and shuts his eyes from looking on evil.*

29. I Timothy 6:9. *But those who desire to be rich fall into temptation, into a snare, into many senseless and harmful desires that plunge people into ruin and destruction.*

CHAPTER SEVEN

The Grave Digger's Story

"Why is corruption so difficult to eradicate?"

The Grave Digger's Story

They usually live in wretched neighborhoods, often in graveyards where they work. Both feared and despised for their work with dead bodies, gravediggers are often disliked by the rest of society, and so they often create a society all their own. Gravediggers can be a source of intelligence about bribery and corruption because they get close to dead bodies, including those known for their corrupt behavior while alive. Sometimes those bodies have stories to tell, stories that gravediggers hear but rarely tell.

Thus, what follows is a rare interview. In it, we learn the story of one gravedigger, a man whose reluctant, weary, sometimes cynical voice nevertheless hides a deep interest in the connection between the way our lives are lived and the way we die. Perhaps his flashes of humor are a result of living too close to death for too long, but certainly not because he does not reflect deeply on the meaning of life and death.

More than most, the gravedigger has witnessed firsthand the many tragic results of bribery and corruption. Dear reader, prepare yourself for the very shocking accounts of the deaths of the wicked, as well the sordid tales of their lives and the tragedies they often leave in their wake.

Your interviewer met our gravedigger shortly after he had completed his day's work. Together, they shared a meal of rice and some unknown meat that some call "bush meat."[*] The stillness of the graveyard set the mood for an interview that was both grave and, in its own way, gracious.

I came to the gravedigger because I had been wrestling long and hard with the question: "Why is corruption so difficult to eradicate?" Since gravediggers hear stories that most of us never hear, I thought this might be the opportunity to learn his answers to this troubling question. His biblical insights made me appreciate that isolation (living in a graveyard) can have its benefits...well, a few.

****

As you know, I am here today to learn why corruption is so hard to eradicate. But, first, maybe you could tell me about some of the people for whom you have dug their grave.

Oh... Why do you need to know?

Well, in order to understand why corruption is like a pest you can ever get rid of. I know that you have stories that the world needs to hear.

Umm… This is awkward. I have never been asked this question. This is a very sensitive topic.

I realize this is difficult…

Are you sure you want to hear my stories? I don't think you know how gruesome this can be.

All right, I admit that I have never delved too deeply into such things, but I want to know. I really do, because the question about the difficulty of eradicating corruption really troubles me.

Okay, I believe you.

I will tell you about a wealthy man who grew up near here in the same kind of poverty that I have experienced. He was young enough to be my son (if I had had one). I barely knew him, but because he was the flashy type, he was hard to miss, especially when he drove by with his entourage of local toughs.

When he was a youngster, he started to follow a well-known local gangster. By the time he was 16 years old or so, he started his own extortion racket. He carried a gun, drove a nice new car, and had a few girlfriends. Some women like all that drama.

I learned to keep my distance from him. He scared me. A few times I saw him carry a loaded gun into a building, and then I would hear gunshots, and he would come out and drive off very fast. He was so afraid that his enemies would get him that he had a couple big guys who acted as his security guards. Mean, cruel,…and nasty.

Earlier this week, he was shot in the city square. Killed. In cold blood. How old do you think he was?

Tell me.

19.

Sobering.

It eats at you, especially when you have been digging graves for almost 25 years like I have.

I find some comfort at a church near here. It's the only group that lets me join them, and, frankly, they make me feel like I belong to a family. We do some Bible study, and singing and praying.

I want to follow up on that. Among those who have died violently because of their involvement in corrupt practices, like this 19-year-old guy, what are some of the stories you hear?

All of us who dig graves here for people under 50 years of age hear stories of violence. They kill others, and then others kill them. Nobody trusts anybody. They pass each other on the street and barely acknowledge each other.

What's worse is that, though these rough, violent guys are the most visible face of corruption, they help to fuel corruption amongst politicians, at the upper end, and the masses of common people, on the lower end.

I told you I have been learning the Bible lately, and a passage in Proverbs 1 makes me think about what I see at least once a week here in the graveyard. Some of these guys are like the man who says, "Come with us; let us lie in wait for blood," and, yet, it says later in that same chapter that "these men lie in wait for their own blood; they set an ambush for their own lives."[2]

The violent die violently.

The interesting thing about that passage in Proverbs is that the goal of the violent is to steal what others have.[3] The end of that chapter says, "Such are the ways of everyone who is greedy for unjust gain; it takes away the life of its possessors."[4]

What is really terrible is that, on occasion, some of these guys are government officials. We rarely bury them, because most of them simply disappear. I imagine the countryside is littered with their buried, government-funded carcasses!

You should see the awful way that many government officials steal from our own people by making illegal demands on them. Thank God, they wouldn't be caught dead here in my graveyard.

116

Like my humor? It's the one good thing about being a gravedigger: No one ever demands a bribe from you (except, of course, for those grisly body snatchers that want to steal corpses). Government officials must think there is some sort of spirit here. They don't want to get near, and so they leave us alone.

I appreciate your confirmation, as a gravedigger, of the link between government officials, violence, and corruption. The prophet Micah said that powerful rulers "hate good and love evil; who tear the skin from my people and the flesh from their bones; who eat my people's flesh, strip off their skin, and break their bones in pieces; who chop them up like meat for the pan, like flesh for the pot."[5] This suggests that some government officials act like cannibals!

I've seen about everything, but that image makes me sick to my stomach…

(The interview was temporarily suspended as the gravedigger waved me away, practically gagging as he turned. I realize that God speaks in such blunt ways through the text of the Bible that at times He shocks us into realizing that what we tolerate is noxious and appalling to Him. The gravedigger came back in several minutes, and sat down again in the evening darkness that was slowly descending on this place of death. He no longer looked white, or so it seemed in the dusk.)

I'm sorry.

It's okay.

Somehow, it never occurred to me that gravediggers would be so sensitive…

You had to speak the truth. I wish that government officials who are corrupt could see how they are very much like cannibals. That's the way the poor experience it! Believe me, we all talk about it. The point is when government officials demand bribes, they threaten violence unless people, especially the powerless, comply.

This takes me back to my basic question about why corruption is so hard to eradicate. You would think that the threat of violence would scare away everyone.

Greed (see Chapter Six) is very powerful. Since it is an idol, according to the Bible, then people will sacrifice their lives. They are so dedicated to it.[6] Violence is just a risk factor for these people.

How about greed, envy, and covetousness? How does that make it hard to eradicate corruption?

When you say "covetousness," you are referring to the desire for what others have, right?

Sure.

The tenth of the 10 Commandments in the Bible says that humans should not desire what their neighbor has.[7] There are lots of dead people in this graveyard who had envy and covetousness written all over them when they died.

So, to answer your question: Greed, envy, and covetousness collaborate to fuel corruption. Greed is all about making money your all-consuming passion, your idol, the thing to which you are supremely devoted. Envy identifies what you want, and covetousness then gives you the determination to take what feeds the greed. Greed says, "I am your idol and I demand to be fed!" Envy says, "I see someone else's possession (money, wife, property etc.) that deserves to be given to the idol." Covetousness says, "I will steal those possessions so that the idol will be fed and worshipped as it demands!"

Virtually all of the biggest players in the corruption racket have massive amounts of greed, envy, and covetousness, and so there is no limit to their corruption, because corruption is really stealing what belongs to others (usually the public) and making it your private possession. Since their idol is an all-consuming passion, and if nothing controls their envy and covetousness, then there is absolutely no limit to how far they will go in order to be corrupt. Because they are envious, they dream about taking what belongs to others, and because they are covetous, they are willing to steal what belongs to others. Greed is the driving passion, the idol that justifies the dreaming and the taking.

I've been thinking about this for a long time.

Do you see why getting rid of corruption is so tough? As a gravedigger, I can tell you that these three (envy, covetousness, and greed)—"The Triple Threat," I call them—are built right into the core of human beings.

This hurts.

The truth *does* hurt, doesn't it?

Part of me wants to gag right now, just like you did a little while ago.

Go ahead.

It's strange, isn't it? Here I am, a gravedigger. You are a journalist, but somehow these deep conversations about profound evil bond us together…in pain.

(With dusk fast approaching, the conversation briefly goes silent as the interviewer and the gravedigger look at each other, as if to say, "We share a human bond deeper than we ever imagined, don't we?")

I've got to say something else. There's another aspect to this that may not be very evident to people who grow up in the West: In many societies, there is tremendous cultural pressure to get all you can when you are in power. In Kenya, they say, "It's our turn to eat."[8] A Liberian raised in his country but now living abroad said of Liberians, "Former public officials or civil servants who do not have booties to show for their period of service are ... decried as failures."[9]

Some people will do anything to even steal another's inheritance, according to the prophet Micah who seemed to be writing about the corrupt in the twenty-first century![10]

When you combine the triple threat of envy, covetousness, and greed with tremendous social pressure to deliver the goods for your ethnic group, your party, or your family, you have a major problem that seems beyond resolution.

I'm thinking now about Achan in Joshua 7. He was a member of the Jewish community that was taking over the Promised Land, but instead of staying away from the plunder, he secretly gathered stolen plunder, including idols. Idolatry and greed, as we discussed, always go together.[11] Achan and his family died a sudden and brutal death for their disobedience.[12]

I've been learning a lot in Proverbs. Here is one that was written not just for Achan but this ought to be a warning to government officials before I see the dead bodies of their family members here at the graveyard: "Whoever is greedy for unjust gain troubles his own household, but he who hates bribes will live."[13]

In the 25 years I have been digging graves, I have seen something that happens to those who love bribes: They have their hearts in their wallets and purses. They store up treasures on earth rather than in heaven.[14] Sometimes their bodies are in closed caskets. On other occasions I have seen their families open the casket and look inside. The huge corpses of dead husbands and fathers have always shocked me. Some died violently, but most died because their diet was fueled by their wealth, and their bodies literally became ill because they overate. Rather than ensuring that everyone in their society had enough to eat, they helped themselves to the luxury that helped kill them.

When I stand far away from the families as they prepare to bury the person they loved, I sometimes wonder if it ever occurred to the dead man that, instead of loving his wallet, he should have invested in people.

Another truth that I discovered, and which the Bible teaches, is that no one can serve two masters.[15] That means that none of us can love our wallets and love God at the same time. Some of these heavily bribed officials who grew fat and ate themselves to death tried to have it both ways. They wanted the bribes and the lifestyle that went with it, but they also wanted to be known as good religious folks. They wanted to love God and love money at the same time.

It can't be done! The love of money is the root of all kinds of evil![16] If you love it, it will eventually destroy you. Those who demand the bribes gorge themselves to death. And they cause great harm to the poor, who are supremely vulnerable to their demands. The poor get thinner as they pay the bribes, while those they bribe get fatter, and both end up in early graves! Corruption kills. (See Chapter One.)

Here is the way Jesus' brother James summed up this situation:

> Behold, the wages of the laborers who mowed your fields, which you kept back by fraud, are crying out against you, and the cries of the harvesters have reached the ears of the Lord of Hosts. You have lived on the earth in luxury and self-indulgence. You have fattened your hearts in a day of slaughter. You have condemned and murdered the righteous person. He does not resist you.[17]

So, violence, envy, covetousness, and greed, combined with social pressures, are powerful reasons why corruption is so hard to wipe out. But, what else makes corruption stay around and haunt us?

If all the dead bodies in this graveyard could speak, they would tell you that corruption destroys trust between people.

It is like an infection that spreads from person to person, and all of a sudden it seems like everyone is infected. People in my society are infected—everyone is infected—with mistrust. It's really hard to know whom you can trust when every secret can be sold for a bribe and when every judge can be purchased likewise. What most people do is to reserve their trust for very close family members. But, even then I have seen people destroyed by close family members who steal property from them.

One of the Hebrew prophets who had his finger on the problem of corruption understood the connection between bribery and the lack of trust between people. Micah wrote that "both hands are skilled in doing evil; the ruler demands gifts, the judge accepts bribes, the powerful dictate what they desire----they all conspire together."[18] Everyone is part of the culture of corruption! So, what is the effect? Two verses later he wrote: "Do not trust a neighbor; put no confidence in a friend. Even with her who lies in your embrace be careful of your words."[19]

Trust is crushed when the truth gets hushed. You look over your back: Who is getting paid to do something that might harm my family or me? Even those who collect bribes can't tell their secret to others, unless it's to another thief with whom they have to conspire.

Broken trust means, in most cases, broken economies, because people with money to invest are afraid to invest it when they know that a lot of the money will be used illegally in bribes.[20] At least that is true for American investors, who must follow very strict American laws against bribery of any type.

Broken trust damages communities, too. Something happened in the early days of the Christian community in Jerusalem that tested this principle. A couple named Ananias and Sapphira sold property, with the agreement that everything they received from the sale would go to the church. But, as corrupt people with greedy hearts, they lied to the leaders of the church and kept part of the money for themselves. God struck them dead because broken trust could not be tolerated in the early days of Christianity. Everyone had to trust everyone in this courageous new faith lest the faith be destroyed from within.[21]

Deep mistrust, which both causes and results from corruption, is like a very deep grave from which trust only rarely emerges. Mistrust perpetuates eternally. Corruption cannot be removed as long as mistrust is so deeply wired into relationships.

When there is mistrust, we want someone to be punished, don't we? Think of whole societies where everyone wants everybody to be punished because no one trusts anyone.

But, when Jesus died on the Cross, all the punishment that each of us deserves was loaded onto Him.[22] That means that we can start trusting each other once again because someone was punished for all the lies that fueled the culture of corruption. Until there is a widespread and serious embrace of Jesus' sacrificial death on our behalf, the problem of mistrust will persist, and that means that corruption will be hard to dislodge.

I see, I see! I appreciate all the time you are taking with me here in the graveyard. We have been talking about how social pressures, greed, envy, covetousness, and mistrust fuel the corrupt culture. But, it occurs to me that what you are saying is that deception is another element wrapped up in this. Deception and mistrust seem to go together, don't they?

True.

Bribery and corruption thrive in darkness. People don't want you to see when they pass bribes to others, and those collecting the bribes don't want others to see, either. We somehow think that if we conceal, then we can deceive others into thinking better of us than they should (see Chapter Two).

Think about our first ancestor. Genesis 2:25 says that Adam and Eve had absolutely nothing to hide.[23] But when the Serpent---Satan---started telling them lies, and they started agreeing with them, they suddenly tied themselves up in sin, which was the first corrupt practice. What happened? They "hid themselves," according to Genesis 3:8. Sin breeds mistrust.

As a gravedigger, I have often thought about a bribe that was associated with deception and death. After Jesus resurrected from the dead, some of those guarding the tomb told the Jewish leaders that Jesus' body suddenly went missing. Fearing that many people believed He could make Himself raise from the dead, the Jewish leaders gave a nice bribe to the guards. They told the guards to tell a false story about why Jesus' body was missing; and, naturally, many people believed the lie that the men were paid to tell about Jesus.[24]

The truth was hushed by money. As long as people are willing to sacrifice the truth for money, corruption continues to choke the good in society, and ultimately weakens and destroys it.[25]

As we have been talking here in this graveyard, I've been thinking about another characteristic of bribery and corruption that explains why it is so difficult to uproot from a society: Bribery and corruption work! The whole thing is tied up with violence, greed, envy, deception, and loss of trust, but the bottom line is that it works.

Money talks, walks, and gets results.

I think that is part of what makes bribery and corruption so powerful. If you want to get something done, if you want to avoid punishment for a crime, if you want to get a contract that will make you and your employees a lot of money, then money is magic: Everyone shows it great respect as if it was a magic wand.

Another story from the Book of Acts illustrates this.[26] A magician by the name of Simon was awed by the miracles that the early church leaders were performing. So he offered lots of money for this ability. Remember that the early church and its leaders were mostly poor people at this time. That's a primary reason why during the early days of the church there was a temporary form of communism where everyone shared what wealth they had.[27]

Why was the Apostle Peter so able to resist the lure of money when he said, "May your money perish with you, because you thought you could buy the gift of God with money!"?[28]

Peter knew that God's economy is a "gift economy," which means that God gives gifts, He doesn't sell them to the highest bidder. If He sold them, then no one but the wealthiest would ever have a chance, would they? The wealthier would get wealthier, and the poor would get poorer, generation after generation.

I never thought about this before.

Neither would I, had I not so much time to think deeply while I dig graves.

God distributes gifts to those He wills.[29] The gifts which He distributes, vocational abilities as well as ministry aptitudes, enable human beings to achieve success that would otherwise be impossible. In some humble way, He has given me gifts.

When God gives gifts, rather than selling them, He is making an announcement to the human race: Everyone should have the ability and opportunity to succeed in their dual purposes as protectors and producers (see Chapter One). His supreme gift was the gift of salvation through the sacrifice of His Son Jesus.[30] No one deserves it, and yet it is offered to everyone!

Think about it: Our corrupt leaders would rather sell their services, wouldn't they? The contractor who offers the biggest kickback, the businessman who offers the biggest house, the community elder who puts the leader's children on the payroll even though they never do anything: These are all exchanges between leaders who demand payment in order to get access to services and privileges. When a society operates this way, the rich get richer and the poor get poorer.

As a gravedigger, that is breaking my heart now.

Mine, too. I am honored that you would take the time to tell me why corruption is so hard to remove from society. For a gravedigger, you are a remarkable teacher!

SUMMARY

Corruption is difficult to get rid of because of:
1. The "Triple Threat" of envy, covetousness, and greed.
    a. Envy focuses desire on what belongs to others.
    b. Covetousness gives the drive to take what belongs to others.
    c. Greed for money is an idol that must be fed by the combination of envy and covetousness.
2. Social pressures (from ethnic groups, family, and party).
3. Mistrust:
    a. Trust is crushed when the truth is hushed.
    b. Damage economies because investment depends upon trust.
4. Violence that sustains the culture of corruption
5. The effectiveness of corruption (it makes many things "work")

STUDY GUIDE

1. What are the many reasons why corruption is so difficult to eradicate? Which one of these is the most prominent and important reason why corruption persists in your society?
2. How has corruption diminished your trust in others?

3. After their painful experience with Ananias and Sapphira (who lied to church leaders, as recorded in Acts 5), what was one step that church leaders took in Chapter Six in order to help restore trust, for this and other reasons? (Note the way they handled leadership.)

4. How do bribes "hush the truth" in your society?

5. For examples of how businesses apply the biblical principles discussed here, I recommend the programs of the Acton Institute in Grand Rapids, Michigan: *www.acton.org*. They also provide scholarships for those who want to participate in their programs.

6. What practical idea for "Taming the Beast" (found in the Appendix) will you and your group deploy as a result of reading this chapter?

NOTES

1. The term "bush meat" refers to the meat of miscellaneous slaughtered wild animals, from bats to monkeys.

2. Proverbs 1:11. *If they say, "Come with us, let us lie in wait for blood; let us ambush the innocent without reason."* Proverbs 1:18. *But these men lie in wait for their own blood; they set an ambush for their own lives.*

3. Proverbs 1:13. *We shall find all precious goods, we shall fill our houses with plunder.*

4. Proverbs 1:19. *Such are the ways of everyone who is greedy for unjust gain; it takes away the life of its possessors.*

5. Micah 3:1-3. *And I said: Hear, you heads of Jacob and rulers of the house of Israel! Is it not for you to know justice?— you who hate the good and love the evil, who tear the skin from off my people and their flesh from off their bones, who eat the flesh of my people, and flay their skin from off them, and break their bones in pieces and chop them up like meat in a pot, like flesh in a cauldron.*

6. Colossians 3:5. *Put to death therefore what is earthly in you: sexual immorality, impurity, passion, evil desire, and covetousness, which is idolatry.*

7. Exodus 20:17. *"You shall not covet your neighbor's house; you shall not covet your neighbor's wife, or his male servant, or his female servant, or his ox, or his donkey, or anything that is your neighbor's."*

8. See Michaela Wrong, *It's Our Turn to Eat: The Story of a Kenya Whistle-Blower* (New York: Harper Perennial, 2010).

9. Stephen Ellis & Gerrie Ter Haar, *Worlds of Power: Religious Thought and Political Practice in Africa* (London: Oxford University Press, 2004), 157.

10. Micah 2: 1-2. *Woe to those who devise wickedness and work evil on their beds. When the morning dawns, they perform it, because it is in the power of their hand They covet fields and seize them, and houses, and take them away; they oppress a man and his house, a man and his inheritance.*

11. See Chapter Six.

12. Joshua 7:20. *And Achan answered Joshua, "Truly I have sinned against the LORD God of Israel, and this is what I did."*

13. Proverbs 15:27. *Whoever is greedy for unjust gain troubles his own household, but he who hates bribes will live.*

14. Matthew 6:19. *"Do not lay up for yourselves treasures on earth, where moth and rust destroy and where thieves break in and steal."*

15. Matthew 6:24. *"No one can serve two masters, for either he will hate the one and love the other, or he will be devoted to the one and despise the other. You cannot serve God and money."*

16. I Timothy 6:10. *For the love of money is a root of all kinds of evils. It is through this craving that some have wandered away from the faith and pierced themselves with many pangs.*

17. James 5:4-6. *Behold, the wages of the laborers who mowed your fields, which you kept back by fraud, are crying out against you, and the cries of the*

harvesters have reached the ears of the Lord of hosts. You have lived on the earth in luxury and in self-indulgence. You have fattened your hearts in a day of slaughter. You have condemned and murdered the righteous person. He does not resist you.

18. Micah 7:3. *Their hands are on what is evil, to do it well; the prince and the judge ask for a bribe, and the great man utters the evil desire of his soul; thus they weave it together.*

19. Micah 7:5. *Put no trust in a neighbor; have no confidence in a friend; guard the doors of your mouth from her who lies in your arms.*

20. cf. Hernando De Soto, *The Mystery of Capital: Why Capitalism Triumphs in the West and Fails Everywhere Else* (New York: Basic Books, 2003).

21. Acts 5:1-11. *But a man named Ananias, with his wife Sapphira, sold a piece of property, and with his wife's knowledge he kept back for himself some of the proceeds and brought only a part of it and laid it at the apostles' feet. But Peter said, "Ananias, why has Satan filled your heart to lie to the Holy Spirit and to keep back for yourself part of the proceeds of the land? While it remained unsold, did it not remain your own? And after it was sold, was it not at your disposal? Why is it that you have contrived this deed in your heart? You have not lied to man but to God." When Ananias heard these words, he fell down and breathed his last. And great fear came upon all who heard of it. The young men rose and wrapped him up and carried him out and buried him. After an interval of about three hours his wife came in, not knowing what had happened. And Peter said to her, "Tell me whether you sold the land for so much." And she said, "Yes, for so much." But Peter said to her, "How is it that you have agreed together to test the Spirit of the Lord? Behold, the feet of those who have buried your husband are at the door, and they will carry you out." Immediately she fell down at his feet and breathed her last. When the young men came in they found her dead, and they carried her out and buried her beside her husband. And great fear came upon the whole church and upon all who heard of these things.*

22. II Corinthians 5:21. *For our sake he made him to be sin who knew no sin, so that in him we might become the righteousness of God.*

23. *And the man and his wife were both naked and were not ashamed.*

24. Matthew 28:11-15. *While they were going, behold, some of the guard went into the city and told the chief priests all that had taken place. And when they had assembled with the elders and taken counsel, they gave a sufficient sum of money to the soldiers and said, "Tell people, 'His disciples came by night and stole him away while we were asleep.' And if this comes to the governor's ears, we will satisfy him and keep you out of trouble." So they took the money and did as they were directed. And this story has been spread among the Jews to this day.*

25. Romans 1:18-32. *For the wrath of God is revealed from heaven against all ungodliness and unrighteousness of men, who by their unrighteousness suppress the truth. For what can be known about God is plain to them, because God has shown it to them. For his invisible attributes, namely, his eternal power and divine nature, have been clearly perceived, ever since the creation of the world, in the things that have been made. So they are without excuse. For although they knew God, they did not honor him as God or give thanks to him, but they became futile in their thinking, and their foolish hearts were darkened. Claiming to be wise, they became fools, and exchanged the glory of the immortal God for images resembling mortal man and birds and animals and creeping things. Therefore God gave them up in the lusts of their hearts to impurity, to the dishonoring of their bodies among themselves, because they exchanged the truth about God for a lie and worshiped and served the creature rather than the Creator, who is blessed forever! Amen. For this reason God gave them up to dishonorable passions. For their women exchanged natural relations for those that are contrary to nature; and the men likewise gave up natural relations with women and were consumed with passion for one another, men committing shameless acts with men and receiving in themselves the due penalty for their error. And since they did not see fit to acknowledge God, God gave them up to a debased mind to do what ought not to be done. They were filled with all manner of unrighteousness, evil, covetousness, malice. They are full of envy, murder, strife, deceit, maliciousness. They are gossips, slanderers, haters of God, insolent, haughty, boastful, inventors of evil, disobedient to parents, foolish, faithless, heartless, ruthless. Though they know God's righteous decree that those who practice such things deserve to die, they not only do them but give approval to those who practice them.*

26. Acts 8:18-19. *Now when Simon saw that the Spirit was given through the laying on of the apostles' hands, he offered them money, saying, "Give me this power also, so that anyone on whom I lay my hands may receive the Holy Spirit."*

27. Acts 2:44-45. *And they devoted themselves to the apostles' teaching and the fellowship, to the breaking of bread and the prayers. And awe came upon every soul, and many wonders and signs were being done through the apostles. And all who believed were together and had all things in common. And they were selling their possessions and belongings and distributing the proceeds to all, as any had need;* Acts 4:32-37. *Now the full number of those who believed were of one heart and soul, and no one said that any of the things that belonged to him was his own, but they had everything in common. And with great power the apostles were giving their testimony to the resurrection of the Lord Jesus, and great grace was upon them all. There was not a needy person among them, for as many as were owners of lands or houses sold them and brought the proceeds of what was sold and laid it at the apostles' feet, and it was distributed to each as any had need. Thus Joseph, who was also called by the apostles Barnabas (which means son of encouragement), a Levite, a native of Cyprus, sold a field that belonged to him and brought the money and laid it at the apostles' feet.*

28. Acts 8:20. *But Peter said to him, "May your silver perish with you, because you thought you could obtain the gift of God with money.*

29. I Corinthians 12:11. *All these are empowered by one and the same Spirit, who apportions to each one individually has he wills.*

30. Ephesians 2:8. *For by grace you have been saved through faith. And this is not your own doing; it is the gift of God.*

CHAPTER EIGHT

The Fly inside the Courtroom

"Why do we want justice in a world full of corruption, and where can we find it?"

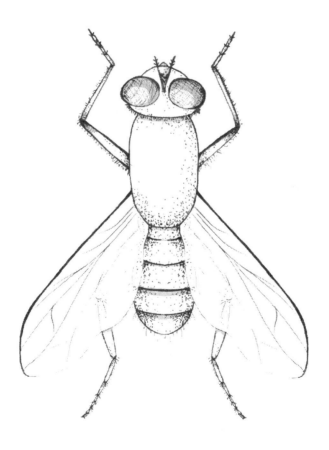

The Fly inside the Courtroom

The primary question that the Bible asks about bribery is this: Can justice be purchased? The experience of most people around the world, from Brazil to Togo to Thailand, is that most judges are more interested in receiving bribes than in ensuring justice. Since political life in the nations is first of all about securing justice, few things can be more important than restoring confidence in judges and their courts. Punishing bribery and its many corruptions is key to restoring that confidence.

Because the matter of justice is so very sensitive, we secretly decided to enlist the services of a particularly observant and reliable informant who inhabits the courtrooms of the world, mostly as a nuisance. Few are aware that the common housefly observes what goes on in courtrooms and in the judge's private chambers where he privately meets with attorneys and their clients.

What follows is a written document based on an alleged recording made by a particularly intelligent fly who saw everything that transpired, the just and the unjust, in one hot and sweaty courtroom. For the sake of everyone involved, including our pesky informant, the city and the nation where the court is located remains a closely guarded secret.

The rampant injustice in this courtroom is shocking. It is, sadly, representative of so many around the world, and it drives a growing impulse to banish injustice from the halls of justice. What surprises us, as you will see, is what this housefly also teaches about the character of a God who, as Judge of the Universe, cannot be bribed.

****

Go...o...d mor...ning. Good morning. You have to forgive me.

You see I am an ordinary fly. I constantly scurry about trying to avoid fly swatters. They are like armed attacks by human hands! They want to kill me. It isn't easy being a common ordinary fly who just wants to go about her business.

And it isn't easy being a defendant in this judge's courtroom. The poor folks who come in seeking justice...why, they must feel like me! They want justice so they can live in peace, but their quest for justice gets tossed aside in the race for money, money, money...

Oops... the mighty judge is quietly slinking in from his private chambers, ready to preside over a court case. I can assure you that everyone in the courtroom expects something other than justice

132

today. That's what happens here, especially when the defendant is a little guy—an ordinary housefly like me, as far as the judge is concerned—up against a rich landowner.

It's all very predictable, and since I fly about (to protect myself, not to make a nuisance), I often get a very impressive view of what goes on behind closed doors. Here's the bottom line: Most of the time, the judge's verdict is determined by what happens in his private chambers. What happens there, frankly, has everything to do with how much money the rich guy is willing to pay the judge for a verdict favorable to his interests.

Swat!!!!!

Wow, that slap of the flyswatter was awfully close! I'd better keep talking as fast as I can, or I won't be able to tell you why justice is so rare in these so-called halls of justice. I also want to tell you why I think you humans desperately seek justice in a corrupt world, as well what I think can be done about it. In so doing, I promise to "tell the whole truth, and nothing but the truth, so help me God!"

Swat!!!!!

This time she missed me by a couple of centimeters! This is a dangerous place to work, and not only for the poor who vainly seek justice here. I need to keep one eye focused on the woman with the flyswatter, or I won't be able to finish my story.

Well, in the case going on before my eyes right now, a poor farmer is bringing a complaint to the judge. His claim is that the rich defendant (a well-known local kingpin[1] who has almost every local politician eating out of his pocket) sent some employees to take over the poor man's farm. Apparently, the rich guy wants to build his third house there. The poor farmer was offered a tiny sum for something worth much, much more. They made him take the pittance, and forced him to sign a sales document that he couldn't read. Now, he and his family are homeless.

This will end predictably. The judge has most definitely met ahead of time with the rich guy's representatives. Money was given to the judge. I've heard they put the money underneath a nice cake that they had delivered to the judge's private chambers about an hour before the court met.

Everything else in the courtroom will be a show that masquerades as justice, and the poor farmer will lose. The judge will claim that the farmer made some technical mistake on the papers that he filed—with the help of a literate relative—several months ago. And the judge will tell him that because of that mistake, he will have to start the process all over again. And then in a few months there will be another court hearing where the whole tragedy gets rehearsed again. The judge will once again find a problem with the poor man's case and then throw it out.

Meanwhile the poor man and his family are homeless for many months, the rich man lives a life of utter ease, the judge gets another beautiful dress for his wife (purchased with currency notes found at the bottom of the cake), and justice flees the courtroom, nowhere to be found.

It's all so predictable, tragic, and unjust.

(Housefly is heard sniffling, as if weeping)[2]

I'm sorry, so sorry. You may think houseflies are heartless nuisances, but even we can't stand the sight of the poor who suffer at the wrong end of a bribe given to a judge.

Why Humans Have a Relentless Quest for Justice

Why do humans agonize over the courtroom injustices suffered by poor farmers and other powerless folks? This is an important question, especially in view of the fact that most people believe in some sort of deity. And if they believe in a deity, then they may likely believe that that deity is just.

However, believing in a deity is not the same thing as living as if God really exists. Many people live as if they are materialists, or naturalists, that is, as people who behave as if matter is all there is. If matter is all that really exists, then there are no obvious reasons why matter—even sophisticated human "matter"—should care about justice. Does the rock scream out, "Give me justice!"? Does the potato plant somehow demand that you give it justice and let it determine whether you get to eat the potatoes it produces?

If matter is all there is, what justifies the human demand for justice in a world full of corruption? Why not let the powerful and the rich have their way? Why not simply close down our courtrooms and announce that the quest for justice was a futile effort, anyway? Why not admit that corruption is just the way things are, and that the fight against it is hopeless?

The reason we demand justice is because the God who made us houseflies and you humans is just and good! Everything He does is always justified in terms of the moral law that is one of his gifts to human beings.

We never need fear that God will change the rules according to His whims, desires, prejudices, or preferences. No, God is an impartial Lawgiver who makes no distinction between rich and poor, powerful and powerless.[3] He is the same God who insisted that Moses appoint only impartial judges, that is, judges unwilling to be motivated by bribes or any other form of prejudice.[4]

This same God, having given humans the responsibility to care for His creation, also established property rights.[5] With respect to this poor man's rights to his property, Moses was very clear that property rights must be honored![6] Nearly a thousand years later, in the religious revival that occurred around 525 BC (when the Jews returned from exile in Babylon), they established a visibly honest and enforceable way to manage the sale and purchase of property: "Fields shall be bought for money, and deeds shall be signed and sealed and witnessed…" (Jeremiah 32:44).

In light of this verse, how can the rich man get away with what he does, except that the judge has been bribed? He sells justice the way that prostitutes sell their bodies!

But, consider this: "Justice makes a difference to individuals mistreated by the culture and institutions of corruption, but what difference does it make to society that God himself is just?"

Swat!!!!!

It's hard work hanging on to this place where the ceiling and the courtroom wall meet each other. That flyswatter is aimed at me every time, and that one was really close. The breeze from the flyswatter nearly caused me to lose my grip, but I know I am safe here because it is hard for them to assault me in this corner crevice.

Thought Experiment: A God Who Could Be Bribed

Anyway, what was I saying? Oh... I was asking the question that you human beings ask: "Does the fact that God is just make a difference in society?" Well, let's think about this by asking another question: "What would happen if God could be bribed?[7] We know that he can't be bribed, according to Deuteronomy 10:17, but as a thought experiment, imagine if He could be bribed.

First, humans wouldn't trust Him. If bribes can manipulate, or change God's will, that means God is for sale. And if He is for sale, that means he, like the judge, has the same relative value as a prostitute, since both can be purchased. Why would you trust someone whose friendships and loves are for sale?

Secondly, and unsurprisingly, you wouldn't trust His claims about justice either. If God's justice is for sale, then honesty is penalized and lawlessness rewarded. The whole idea of fair and impartial justice, the foundation of the modern court system, would be null and void.

Thirdly, God's unconditional love (a central Christian teaching)[8] conflicts with the idea of a God who could be bribed. If he could be bribed, then He would be obligated to offer His services to the one who purchased them, not to the one to whom God chooses to show charitable love, asking nothing in return. So, if God could be bribed, then people would have little ability to both receive and express love without conditions.

Fourthly, science would be impossible. If God could manipulate scientific laws to satisfy someone who gives Him an adequate bribe, then science would be an unpredictable disaster.[9] Without science, technology would remain primitive and everyone poorer.

Finally, if He needed bribes, what does this say about the claim that God is the Sovereign over the Universe? That is, any need on His part would mean that He is less than sufficient in Himself and thus not sufficient to create the entire Universe. This means God would be impotent to create because He needs it for His existence.

A bribe-taking deity and His justice could not be trusted, love would be conditional, science (and its technological fruits) would be impossible, and He could not have created the Universe since by definition He would be in need of it.

The Larger Cost to our Mandate to Protect and Produce

And since God can't be bribed,[10] why do humans let themselves be bribed? This is no small question. When humans accept bribes, they diminish God. And why is that the case? As God's image-bearers, human beings were created to reflect His glory back to Him. That is, by reflecting His glory back to Him, human beings draw greater attention to Him and His works. But when humans accept bribes, they act completely out of character with the God who made them, and so, instead of glorifying Him, they make Him look like just another one of the many village spirits that demand bribes (offerings) in order to grant blessings or harm their enemies.[11]

In addition to diminishing God, another reason the Bible condemns bribery is because it undermines justice.[12] This is precisely what is at stake in every courtroom, and the tragedy is that justice can be bought in so many of them. Remember, when bribes undermine justice, they also undermine the just rewards, or natural blessings, that come with protecting God's creation and producing those things that make human life worth living.

It's simple when you think about it. A corrupt businessman buys off a government official who is responsible for protecting the environment, and then hires men to destroy or somehow ruin the environment (for example, massive clear-cutting destroys large tracts of virgin forest). This means that, in this particular country, the reward for taking care of the environment through wise stewardship is very small, whereas there is great benefit to recklessly using, or raping the environment.

Consider another example. You create high-quality roads, and your competitor, who creates very cheap and shoddy roads, bribes a government official to give him the road-building contract. What does this mean for your God-given mandate, or responsibility, to produce the things that make human beings flourish? The cost of producing high-quality roads that last a long time and which don't destroy the citizens' vehicles is much higher than the cost of producing cheap quality roads. If the citizens had the high-quality roads that you provide, they would be able to speedily go to and from their jobs. That means enhanced productivity. But they won't be as productive because your shoddy road-building competitor bribed the government. Furthermore, drivers would waste less fuel on your high-quality road instead of wasting fuel by having to slow down and speed up around all the craters in the shoddy road. That means that drivers will be able to better protect the environment.

Do you see how bribery undercuts the mandate God has given you humans to protect and to produce? We flies have no such mandate, but we can only imagine your privilege as humans for having been given such great responsibility. And to think that so many of you sell the privilege for a cheap and dirty bribe!

(Even though you human beings may be our mortal enemies, especially when you are at the other end of a flyswatter, nevertheless, we still have compassion for you. We houseflies see clearly that you live so much farther from your original design than you can ever imagine.)

How Bribery Makes Justice Costly

Here are three reasons that injustice purchased by a bribe is a terrible thing.

First of all, bribery distorts the efforts of otherwise good people.[13] Good and wise judges suddenly lose their passion for justice when a bribe is offered. The Bible says that bribes "blind" people, and "twists the words of the innocent."[14] They want to improve their societies, but their goals and strategies are completely confused by bribes because money "talks," as Americans sometimes say. Bribes muddle and confuse the case for justice.

Secondly, bribes breed chaos instead of stability.[15] A stable society ensures that everyone knows what are the rules, what are the predictable penalties for violating the rules, and who is responsible for assigning the penalties. A stable society is a predictable society, and most people will choose a predictable society over one where chaos and anarchy rule. In a predictable society, you know that if your neighbor steals from you, then the judge will assign a predictable penalty that motivates your neighbor to stop stealing. But, when justice can be purchased with a bribe, your neighbor can avoid the penalty by paying the judge. And, in turn, your neighbor has no reason to stop stealing from you. This means that, if given a choice, you will flee that society for one where the rule of law is maintained and predictably and fairly applied.

Finally, bribery's third cost to justice is the terror it creates among the poor.[16] When those who set and enforce rules for justice fall in love with bribes, their concerns change. Instead of being concerned for the welfare of all their people, they spend their waking hours concerned only for their own welfare. When the prophet Isaiah said that they "chase after gifts,"[17] he reminded me of the way we houseflies chase around after food: landing wherever we can to get a meal, and not the least concerned for those whom we make miserable. Imagine that! Your leaders are just like us houseflies!

But, you ask: "Since corruption imposes such terrible costs on justice, don't those who threaten justice and destroy so many lives deserve judgment?"

I am honored that you would ask such a gigantic question of such a tiny fly as me! You must think so highly of me...

Swat!!!!

Why Judgment and Accountability Are Important

I guess not! You respect me and my ability to buzz around your lives. And so you humans go to great efforts to eradicate me! That's called, in your language, "judgment."

(The housefly giggles for several minutes. She has successfully outwitted a human-held flyswatter for the 157th time. Even houseflies take pride in such evasive skills!)

Judgment is what we deserve for the way we live our lives. When corrupt judges daily destroy others' lives, merely because of bribes, then they should be held accountable and must pay a price for their evil behavior. When public officials are held accountable for their corruption, and when they are either sent to prison (a form of punishment called retribution) or pay back what they have stolen (or some other punishment), the net effect is to restore

139

confidence and trust in government.

Speaking of restitution (the term for paying back what has been stolen), the Bible teaches that it needs to be paid by those who benefit from corruption. The Bible teaches that when extortion (demanding money for unwanted services like protection) takes place, the money extorted[18] has to be paid back, along with an additional 20% and some type of costly offering to God.[19] Payment of restitution (including the 20% penalty) not only redresses the wrong, but it also warns those who hope to benefit from corruption in the future.

So, corrupt officials, including corrupt judges, must be held accountable and must pay the price for their evil, just as the violent and corrupt men and women did during Noah's lifetime (see Chapter Three). But, the fact is, from what I hear amongst flies that circulate around the globe and collect information about human beings, there is little or no accountability anywhere on the planet, except in North American and, recently, parts of China. Corrupt officials get off without punishments, and so other public officials learn that they too can get away without punishment.

As I mentioned, the two exceptions to this rule are, first, Western countries like the USA. Their legal system, in its origin, depends upon the idea of impartial law, an idea they learned from their Bibles. Americans actually drove out of office one of their presidents who, in the 1970s, was corrupt.[20] China is another country that currently demands some accountability from its public officials. Their leader, Xi Jinping, is determined to show that his Communist Party is worthy of the loyalty of the Chinese people.[21] Unlike Western countries, the standard of accountability is not objective law, but the will of the supreme leader.

In most countries, however, few public officials need fear punishment for their wrongs. Why is this? Are there inadequate systems for guaranteeing justice? Do the courts believe they must serve the interests of the officials in the government rather than justice itself (and the God who is the author of justice)? It may be a confused idea about God's mercy. It may be a lack of virtue. It may be all of the above.

Swat!!!!

Another close call, for the 158th time!

Why God's Mercy Should Not Be Used to Overlook Judgment on Corruption

Does God's mercy preclude your human responsibility to hold accountable and punish those who engage in corruption?

Remember, first, that God's mercy toward human beings came at a cost: the death of His Son. "God so loved the world that He gave his only Son…"[22] When Jesus Christ died to save people from their sins, he assumed the punishment for their sin, a punishment that should have been poured out on all people.[23] So, dear humans, let me say this clearly: If public officials expect to be shown mercy, as humans are shown mercy through the saving death of Jesus Christ, they have to expect that someone will have to be punished. Why should someone else be punished for the sins committed by public officials?

One of the great Roman Catholic popes wrote: "In no passage of the Gospel does forgiveness, or mercy as its source, mean indulgence toward evil, toward scandal, toward injury or insult."[24]

Besides the fact that the Bible teaches that someone has to be punished for law breaking, note that the purpose of mercy is always to provoke personal transformation in the life of the corrupt person. God is just when he displays mercy, and expects that the one who experiences mercy will fully repent and make restitution, along with an appropriate penalty.

Showing mercy should never ever be an excuse for refusing to punish a government official for being corrupt. It does not matter whether the public official is from your church, your tribe, or from your family; if they are corrupt, they should be tried and convicted. If convicted, they should be punished. No society will make progress toward ridding itself of corruption if it does not punish the corrupt, demanding, at minimum, restitution.

Those who are corrupt deserve to have the opportunity to be restored to society as forgiven sinners, much as the Apostle Paul consoled the church in Corinth.[25] By paying back some of which they have taken, such officials can give proof that they are sincere about changing for the better.

The Fly inside the Courtroom

Swat!!!!

Oh, how I would love some human being to show mercy to me!!! It's tough being a fly, and having to teach human beings about how to find justice in a world full of corruption.

I know that you probably wonder how public officials will be held accountable. That has always been the problem. Public officials, namely judges and prosecuting attorneys, are expected to hold other public officials, whether judges, government ministries, the military, or bureaucrats accountable for their behavior. Do you think that will happen? Hardly!!![26]

But, there are several organizations that exist to help you citizens hold them accountable. The first is called the International Justice Mission.[27] They have a team of dedicated investigators and lawyers, who have the skill and the determination to, at least in many cases, hold public officials accountable to their own laws. That brings up another organization: International Criminal Court.[28] This court, which has been authorized by nations around the world, aims to hold public officials accountable when no one else does so. This young organization, begun in 1998, will need many years before they achieve their full capacity to make public officials pay for their crimes,

The judge is nearly finished with the case. The unjust outcome is assured. Rather than justice, which the judge is supposed to "carefully" undertake according to the Bible, instead, injustice has reigned![29] But, here in this tiny space where walls meet ceilings, I ask the question: "Does the judge have any idea how God sees him?" The prophet Jeremiah, weary and exhausted by corruption everywhere he looked, asked, "To defraud a person in a lawsuit— the Lord does not approve of such things!"[30] Judges are not immune to God's judgment.

But, in my very small world, I cannot help but ask God what the prophet Habakkuk also asked Him: "Why do you tolerate wrong?"[31]

Swat!!!!

Umph…That caught my tail. I wonder if some of your judges need a flyswatter used on them.

What do you think?

SUMMARY

1. God's justice is the basis for our ideas about justice.
2. If God could be bribed:
   a. He and His justice would not be trusted.
   b. Love would be conditional.
   c. Science (and its technological fruits) would be impossible.
   d. He could not have created the universe.
3. Bribery undermines the just rewards for protecting God's creation and producing those things that make human life worth living.
4. Bribes undermine justice by:
   a. Muddling its case.
   b. Removing its predictability.
   c. Terrorizing the poor.
5. Judgment on corruption can take two major forms:
   a. Retribution (often involving a prison sentence).
   b. Restitution.
6. Judgment and accountability are important to justice in a corrupt world through:
   a. Restoring confidence and trust in government.
   b. Redressing the wrong, but also by standing as a warning to those who want to take part in corruption in the future.
7. Why God's mercy should not be used to overlook judgment on corruption:
   a. Jesus Christ had to pay the penalty for our law breaking, which means that someone still had to pay a penalty. Why not those who are corrupt?
   b. God is just when he displays mercy, and expects that the one who experiences mercy will fully repent and make restitution, along with a requisite penalty.

STUDY GUIDE

1. Why does the case against corruption have everything to do with God's character?
2. How does bribery undermine the "protect and produce" mandate that God has given human beings?
3. How do bribes affect justice?
4. Discuss the ways that bribes are used to undermine justice in your society.
5. Why is it important to hold the corrupt accountable for their corrupt activities? How might some people try to appeal to God's mercy as an argument against holding people accountable for crimes of corruption?
6. What practical idea for "Taming the Beast" (found in the Appendix) will you and your group deploy as a result of reading this chapter?

NOTES

1. A person who is essential to the success of an operation or organization.

2. While this transcription employs some imaginative features—like weeping flies—it is true that flies have surprisingly human-like traits. One professor from an American university claims that a "pet fly" once slept on his computer, night after night (true story)!

3. Leviticus 19:15. *"You shall do no injustice in court. You shall not be partial to the poor or defer to the great, but in righteousness shall you judge your neighbor."*

4. Deuteronomy 1:17. *You shall not be partial in judgment. You shall hear the small and the great alike. You shall not be intimidated by anyone, for the judgment is God's. And the case that is too hard for you, you shall bring to me, and I will hear it.'*

5. Genesis 1:26-28. *So God created man in his own image, in the image of God he created him; male and female he created them. And God blessed them. And God said to them, "Be fruitful and multiply and fill the earth and*

subdue it, and have dominion over the fish of the sea and over the birds of the heavens and over every living thing that moves on the earth."

6. Deuteronomy 19:14. *"You shall not move your neighbor's landmark, which the men of old have set, in the inheritance that you will hold in the land that the LORD your God is giving you to possess."* Deuteronomy 27:17. *"'Cursed be anyone who moves his neighbor's landmark.' And all the people shall say, 'Amen.'.*

7. The section that follows is abbreviated from my unpublished paper "How Bribery and Corruption Stunt Society."

8. Romans 5:8. *But God shows his love for us in that while we were still sinners, Christ died for us.*

9. It is true that when God performs miracles, He is somehow briefly suspending some existing scientific laws that He created. He does it, however, temporarily and briefly, after which the natural laws resume their former state.

10. See Chapter One.

11. See Chapter Four.

12. Exodus 23:8. *And you shall take no bribe, for a bribe blinds the clear-sighted and subverts the cause of those who are in the right.* Deuteronomy 1:17. *You shall not be partial in judgment. You shall hear the small and the great alike. You shall not be intimidated by anyone, for the judgment is God's. And the case that is too hard for you, you shall bring to me, and I will hear it.'* Deuteronomy 16:18-20. *"You shall appoint judges and officers in all your towns that the LORD your God is giving you, according to your tribes, and they shall judge the people with righteous judgment. You shall not pervert justice. You shall not show partiality, and you shall not accept a bribe, for a bribe blinds the eyes of the wise and subverts the cause of the righteous. Justice, and only justice, you shall follow, that you may live and inherit the land that the LORD your God is giving you."* II Chronicles 19:7. *"Now then, let the fear of the LORD be upon you. Be careful what you do, for there is no injustice with the LORD our God, or partiality or taking bribes."* Isaiah

5:22-23. *Woe to those who are heroes at drinking wine, and valiant men in mixing strong drink, who acquit the guilty for a bribe, and deprive the innocent of his right!*

13. Deuteronomy 16:19. *You shall not pervert justice. You shall not show partiality, and you shall not accept a bribe, for a bribe blinds the eyes of the wise and subverts the cause of the righteous.*

14. Exodus 23:8 (NIV). *"Do not accept a bribe, for a bribe blinds those who see and twists the words of the innocent."*

15. Proverbs 29:4. *By justice a king builds up the land, but he who exacts gifts tears it down.*

16. Isaiah 1:23. *Your princes are rebels and companions of thieves. Everyone loves a bribe and runs after gifts. They do not bring justice to the fatherless, and the widow's cause does not come to them.* and Isaiah 3:15. *"What do you mean by crushing my people, by grinding the face of the poor?" declares the Lord GOD of hosts.*

17. Isaiah 1:23. *Your princes are rebels and companions of thieves. Everyone loves a bribe and runs after gifts. They do not bring justice to the fatherless, and the widow's cause does not come to them.*

18. It is correct to assume that what should be paid back is the original value of what was stolen plus its additional investment value. Thus, if someone is forced to pay 10,000 *naira* (Nigerian) through extortion, then what should be returned is the 10,000 plus the additional wealth that would have been generated had the sum of *naira* been invested. The additional 20% is a penalty, whereas the offering to God is the basis for reconciliation with God.

19. Leviticus 6:4. *If he has sinned and has realized his guilt and will restore what he took by robbery or what he got by oppression or the deposit that was committed to him or the lost thing that he found.* cf. Numbers 5:5-10. *And the LORD spoke to Moses, saying, "Speak to the people of Israel, When a man or woman commits any of the sins that people commit by breaking faith with the LORD, and that person realizes his guilt, he shall confess his sin that he has committed. And he shall make full restitution for his wrong,*

adding a fifth to it and giving it to him to whom he did the wrong. But if the man has no next of kin to whom restitution may be made for the wrong, the restitution for wrong shall go to the LORD for the priest, in addition to the ram of atonement with which atonement is made for him. And every contribution, all the holy donations of the people of Israel, which they bring to the priest, shall be his. Each one shall keep his holy donations: whatever anyone gives to the priest shall be his."

20. Richard Nixon, the 37th American president (1968-1974).

21. President Xi may also have other objectives in his anti-corruption campaign.

22. John 3:16a. *"For God so loved the world, that he gave his only Son…"*

23. I Peter 2:24. *"All flesh is like grass and all its glory like the flower of grass. The grass withers, and the flower falls."*

24. Pope John Paul II.

25. II Corinthians 2:6-11. *For such a one, this punishment by the majority is enough, so you should rather turn to forgive and comfort him, or he may be overwhelmed by excessive sorrow. So I beg you to reaffirm your love for him. For this is why I wrote, that I might test you and know whether you are obedient in everything. Anyone whom you forgive, I also forgive. Indeed, what I have forgiven, if I have forgiven anything, has been for your sake in the presence of Christ, so that we would not be outwitted by Satan; for we are not ignorant of his designs.*

26. See Chapter Five.

27. *www.ijm.org.*

28. *http://www.icc-cpi.int/en_menus/icc/Pages/default.aspx.*

29. II Chronicles 19:7. *"Now then, let the fear of the LORD be upon you. Be careful what you do, for there is no injustice with the LORD our God, or partiality or taking bribes."*

30. Lamentations 3:36 (NET Bible). *To defraud a person in a lawsuit—the Lord does not approve of such things!*

31. Habakkuk 1:3. *Why do you make me see iniquity, and why do you idly look at wrong? Destruction and violence are before me; strife and contention arise.*

CHAPTER NINE

At the Marketplace:
The Weigh Scale Tells All

"How does corruption weaken economies?"

When we think of corruption, this is usually what we have in mind: Currency or other valuables are exchanged with someone (often a government official) who has the power to grant access to a given service (such as a license to do business). Government is the central hub for corruption.

At the Marketplace: The Weigh Scale Tells All

Dare we hope that the marketplace is, by contrast, free of corruption? Lively, crowded, always bustling with energetic sellers and their customers, the marketplaces of the world are, unfortunately, no haven from human sinfulness. The astonishing power of greed fuels simple and sophisticated efforts to cheat and steal. In this chapter, we focus on a simple but widespread corrupt practice that involves weigh scales and any other instrument used to measure the value of a service or product.

What is the function of the weigh scale? It measures the weight of whatever is being sold or purchased. In turn, weight determines how much a customer should pay for the product or service. But, the scale can be manipulated, so that customers are led to believe they are receiving more products and services than they are actually receiving.

We discovered a particularly articulate and insightful weigh scale in an unnamed Latin American country who was more than happy to tell us all about corruption in the marketplace. As we will discover, his insights have real implications for whether or not national economics barely survive or thrive.

****

Being a weigh scale is hard work!

Many of us work seven days a week, often 16 hours each day, amidst the clutter and the noise of the marketplace. No one thanks us for weighing things that people want to buy or sell, even though we try to provide a reliable and accurate measure of the weight of a given product that is for sale. With that information, the seller and buyer come to agreement on what is a fair price for the product being sold. It could be chickens, peas, mangoes, olives, cauliflower, corn, beans, tomatoes, rice, or any of a thousand other products.

We weigh scales love to provide accurate measures! That's what we were created to do, and we love to do it to the best of our abilities!

But, we cannot control our owners, the shopkeepers. Many of them manipulate us in order to deceive customers. When shopkeepers change the settings on weigh scales, the results are inaccurate. Our scales say one thing, but the reality is that customers are getting less than the scales show. Thus, our owners make more money for the same amount of product (or they pay less than they should for some product that they want).

In other words, our owners use us in order to cheat their

customers. With no choice in the matter, I am an innocent partner in corruption!

Another way that shopkeepers cheat people is by mixing in false substances or ingredients, even though they may claim to be "pure." Grain elevator operators will sometimes mix water with the grain that they ship in rail cars, while manufacturers sometimes mix cheap or damaging substances into expensive medicines and food products. People think they are receiving the full amount of desired goods, when, in fact, they are not. I'm sure you are not surprised to discover that God condemns this practice as well![1]

We weigh scales deplore the deception, but we have no choice; we are the slaves of our masters, the shopkeepers, and so we become unwilling conspirators in corruption.

Oomph!!!!

There goes another pile of green beans. How much they weigh determines how much the customer will have to pay, but, as I already told you, I have been tampered with. Thus, my scales show more weight than is actually on my scale.

Most people in this society eagerly condemn government officials who make themselves personally rich at public expense. But what about the private shopkeepers like my boss? There are hundreds in this market, and very, very few have not altered their scales.

Oomph!!!!

Whew...sometimes these loads hit like a ton of bricks. That load weighed in as the heaviest load placed on my weigh scale all day.

While I am very cynical about the dishonesty of shopkeepers, there are some customers who seem to have access to God. One is a pastor who regularly frequents our shop, and I often overhear him when he engages my owner in conversation.

He talks about God's kindness, mercy, and love. And some days he talks about God's judgment.

One day he said that his afternoon appointment was canceled.

He wanted to know if my owner, the shopkeeper, would mind him staying around the shop. As someone who really knew how to care for the members of his church, he hoped to see some of them in the shop.

But, he also had another reason: He wanted my owner to start thinking about God's approach to business.

"Did you know that Jesus Christ spoke more about money than almost any other subject in the New Testament?" he asked.

Barely waiting for my owner to answer, the pastor went on: "Did you know that the Bible teaches that dishonest weigh scales are forbidden?[2] They are forbidden because they completely violate the character of God, who has never cheated His people. God is completely trustworthy, and thus He deserves the trust of His people."

"I didn't know that," my owner responded. He obviously wanted to change the subject, but the pastor was firm and insistent.

"There is a second thing the Bible teaches about business: Dishonest scales deserve God's judgment."[3] The air was getting tense. Secretly, I cheered for the pastor...

Oomph!

That was a big load! It almost broke me. Well, now let me get back to the pastor's conversation with my boss, who was starting to sweat and shuffle around, looking for a place of escape.

"In fact, God is very passionate about dishonest scales: Proverbs 11:1 says that he 'hates' them! The Bible also says that those who use dishonest scales and weights are disgusting to Him. Using dishonest scales is utterly and completely opposed to everything that God is, and dishonest business people and their transactions invite God's complete judgment.[4] One biblical prophet asks, using the voice of God: 'Shall I acquit a man with dishonest scales, with a bag of false weights?'[5] How would you answer the prophet?"

You could hear noise elsewhere in the marketplace, but in this spot there was complete silence as the pastor silently peered at my boss.

"Uh...I have something I forgot. I must go fetch it right now!

See you later, pastor," my boss uttered as he hastily backed toward another section of the market.

For his part, the pastor waved goodbye with a gentle smile on his face. I cheered secretly. The pastor's question was aimed for the heart. I think it reached its destination.

Oomph!

It's my job: I'm the weigh scale. Happy to serve, but some days...

As I think about corruption in the marketplace, I realize that pastor answered one of questions: Does God care about this, and, if so, what does He have to say about it?

Four Forms of Marketplace Corruption

But, now I have another question: What are the different forms of marketplace, or business corruption? And what terms are used to describe those different forms of corruption?

I listen to the radios that constantly blare in our market, and I have concluded that there are at least three common forms of business corruption. The first is known by the simple term *fraud*, which refers to employing deception with the goal of stealing from another. Or, in our case, we sell to customers products or services that are less than the value they pay for. There are many other forms of fraud, such as bank fraud, insurance fraud, and wage fraud.[6] They all use seemingly legitimate tools (such as loans, insurance policies, or paychecks) as ways to steal from the innocent. The corrupt have endless tools for moving illicit funds to their pockets.

The second way that businesspeople dishonestly "tip" the scales in their favor is by *collusion*.[7] This refers to businesses in the same market sector reducing competition amongst themselves so that they can drive up the charges for their products and services. For example, if all the paper distributors in a country collude, they will agree to divide up the market according to types of paper, for example. This often involves some form of price-fixing. From their perspective as businesses, this is a way to ensure high levels of profitability. For those to whom they sell their products, since the competitive dimension is missing, product quality will decrease, prices will increase, or both. Collusion is another example of business corruption, and, as one businessman said recently: "Corruption and collusion is the biggest weapon of mass destruction on the earth today!"

Given human beings' creative capacities, there are many other forms of business corruption, including a third one that usually involves employees stealing from their employers. This is called *embezzlement*. Embezzlers steal money from their employers and redirect it to their personal accounts. American newspapers teem with accounts of trusted bookkeepers who silently and secretly steal from employers so that they can pay personal debts, purchases gifts for their children, and gamble in hopes of striking it rich.

And then a fourth and more common version of business corruption involves *shoplifting*, whereby customers and employees take goods and services without paying for them. For some people, the allure of a piece of clothing or high-tech gear sends a signal to the idol of greed, an idol that demands to be fed at almost any cost. Stuffed inside a purse or a bag, the product disappears, unpaid-for. In the USA alone, shoplifting costs retailers over $33 billion each year.[8] Corruption is costly!

These and other means of business fraud result in higher costs for legitimate and honest users of the products and services. If you know your Bible (I am rare among weigh scales in that I know biblical teaching), you will recognize that these forms of business corruption involve, to one extent or another, breaking the Eighth and Ninth commandments *(You shall not steal. You shall not bear false witness against your neighbor.)* in order to also successfully break the Tenth commandment *(You shall not covet your neighbor's house…or anything that is your neighbor's).*

I fear for the shopkeeper who owns me, as he has defrauded many people by manipulating me. Whereas God "hates" dishonest scales (as we saw earlier), some people, like my boss, literally "love" to defraud others, so say the biblical prophets Amos and Hosea.[9]

It's hard to find anyone who would say that he should be allowed to freely cheat the way that he has. Some people have damned him in their hearts. If I am not mistaken, God will do likewise.

Negative Effects of Bribery and Corruption on Economies

Well, now let me share with you another question that I have been thinking about. It's one thing to think about the ways that business corruption manifests itself, but how does corruption affect whole economies?

Thanks to radios that have been tuned to wonderful stations like BBC, I've heard about years of research conducted by economists in the USA and Europe. They've learned many powerful lessons. The essential lesson is summed up in this sentence from two American scholars: "Research indicates that higher levels of corruption significantly reduce GNP growth rates."[10] That is another way of saying that bribery and corruption diminish economies. If that is true, how does it happen?

First, bribery and corruption stunt societies because bribes divert money away from normal economic activity that promotes economic growth. Imagine a policeman has stopped you and is demanding a bribe with the threat of taking your vehicle from you (around the world, this happens perhaps thousands of times daily). If you must pay a bribe of US$30, then that money is no longer available for you to purchase your family's food during the next week.

By contrast, in a just society bribes are rare. In those societies, people will be able to use those funds to support their families. Because that is the case, their economic activity will in turn drive other economic activity, which makes everyone richer and better able to flourish. In those societies where bribes must be paid in order to keep the vehicle, then those funds not only cannot be used to purchase food, but the absence of economic activity in turn undercuts the possibility of other economic activity. Everyone becomes poorer, as a result.

Secondly, people are forced to participate in underground economies when corruption is prevalent. By this, I mean economic transactions (like buying food) must take place in hidden places, sometimes called the "black market."

Contracts can't be enforced underground because governments, in fact, fail to enforce contracts above ground.[11] That is, when governments don't insist on just transactions in the marketplace, then people prefer transactions in the underground economy where government has no power to tax or regulate. Since taxes can't be collected from the underground economy, governments miss that revenue and, in turn, use this fact to help justify government-driven extortion. It's a vicious cycle.

Thirdly, corruption reduces the willingness to take financial risks when starting businesses. If regulation is lax, bribes must be paid to win favor from government officials is unknown, then there is less desire to start high-risk businesses that could offer badly-needed jobs. Most people don't realize that most of the economic growth in the USA has been a result of great risk-taking by investors. They took smart risks because they knew they could trust the legal system in the USA to be relatively just.

Fourthly and finally, extensive corruption enhances the quality of the government labor force while simultaneously reducing the quality of the private labor force. When the benefits of institutionalized corruption are great, the best-educated will aspire to government positions that entitle them to receive large bribes. Sadly, the very people best-positioned to intelligently grow businesses that hire large numbers of people are siphoned away from private industry to government positions that do not create new wealth. The society as a whole suffers because fewer high-quality, high-employment businesses are created, and, thus, the economy is weaker than it would be otherwise.

Corruption diverts money so that it can't be used to grow the economy, it fosters underground economies, it reduces risk-taking by entrepreneurs, and weakens the quality of labor that is needed for the private sector to generate economic growth.

Oomph!

All day long, I have these interruptions as people load their produce on my weigh scale. As you can tell, what I love about my job, however, is the tremendous opportunities to think about how economies work, and the effect of bribery and corruption on them. I hope you enjoy learning these basic lessons!

Oomph!!!!

There goes another load; this time it's a bag of rice.

Benefits of Honesty in Business

Since I am a realist, not only do I want to be aware of what can go wrong when corruption is prevalent, but I also want to be aware of the benefits of a non-corrupt society. What are the marks of a non-corrupt society where people are honest with one another? They keep their word by fulfilling contracts, even when they may lose money.[12] They are transparent, always telling the truth even when it is not pleasant.[13] And, finally, they refund customers when they produce bad products or services.

Honesty breeds honesty, with the result that businesses will want to take risks and invest. Knowing they can trust the government officials, contractors, and lending institutions means that uncertainty is reduced. Rationally, they conclude that the prospects of making a profit are good. Thus, jobs will be created, and the economy will begin to flourish simply because of business activity that results from a business environment shaped by honesty. Second, those who are honest can expect to live long lives where they can enjoy and wisely utilize the wealth that has been generated in their high-trust society. They live till old age because they don't unnecessarily create enemies (unlike dishonest shopkeepers), but also because God loves to favor those who honor and reflect His character.[14] Those who are honest inevitably glorify Him and His character, in part by treating other human beings as fellow image bearers of God instead of victims who can be easily duped by rigging dishonest weigh scales, for example. Human beings, even as sinners, want to be treated with the dignity and respect that befits those made in the image of a holy and just God.[15]

Oomph!!!!

A lot of people are buying bread, milk, eggs, and hummus today. I am getting a good workout!

Public Standards that Can Encourage Honesty and Economic Growth

Can public standards be instituted and enforced so that people will be more honest than they would otherwise be? The Bible talks a lot about this, believe it or not!

For example, when the Promised Land was divided among the Jewish tribes, the process completely excluded bribery.[16] Once tribal and family boundaries were set, there was a transparent and enforceable method that ensured no one moved the "boundary stones" that indicated the boundaries between properties.[17]

God very wisely set up a system for fair distribution of land, and He even accounted for special conditions. For example, one tribe (the Levites) had no property, so God created a system of *tithing* to make sure everyone else shared some of their created wealth (largely agricultural production) with the Levites. Because of his earlier courage and his wholehearted dedication to God, Caleb received a special grant of property, but once again this was all done in a very transparent way (by virtue of the fact that God included this in the biblical text). Nothing was done secretly![18] Joshua was the very last to receive a land allotment, even though he was the hero who led the victorious military effort to bring the Israelites into the Promised Land.[19]

A Brief Case Study: Singapore the Non-Corrupt State

As a weigh scale, I'm always looking for examples of nations where corruption is largely absent. Here's one that I learned about recently: Singapore, a tiny but extraordinarily prosperous nation in Southeast Asia.

What made that nation one of the world's 10 least-corrupt nations (according to Transparency International)? And why is it so free of corruption, when the nations around it are so corrupt? The simple answer: Lee Kuan Yew, the nation's founder. He founded the nation in 1960 (as a breakaway state from what is today Malaysia).

Having studied at Cambridge University in Great Britain during the 1940s, Mr. Yew realized that the relative success of the English economy was in part due to its absence of corruption. When people could trust weigh scales like me, then they began to trust their political leaders, and vice versa. With immense energy and determination, shortly after Singapore became independent, Yew confronted the corruption among pre-existing authorities. Simply put, he did what we mentioned in our previous discussion. His strategy was threefold: 1) He relentlessly threatened government employees with jail if they were found to be corrupt; 2) He increased government employee salaries so that they would not be tempted to engage in corrupt practices; and 3) He insisted on a public, transparent process for resolving charges of government corruption.

The result of an exceedingly clean government? Businesses want to set up shop in large numbers, resulting in thriving marketplaces where weigh scales like yours truly can thrive and be free of the corruption we experience in most marketplaces of the world. Today, Singapore is one of the world's richest countries when measured in terms of per capita income. The connection between their prosperous economy and their very low levels of corruption is too obvious to ignore.

Prime Minister Yew tamed the beast, but he did it at a cost. To accomplish his goal of a non-corrupt society, Prime Minister Yew sacrificed individual liberties. Thus, many people consider Singapore a "benevolent dictatorship."

By contrast, a major claim of the author of this book is that Jesus Christ can clean up the corruption in a society while *also* ensuring freedom and liberty (see Chapter Twelve). That's something worth exploring!

Oomph!

Oh, my… I am ready for this day to come to an end. It's been long, and, as you know, I've had to tell you my story without drawing the attention or arousing the anger of my owner. If he had any idea, he would be furious!

I only wish that he knew what I have come to realize very slowly, and that is that God sees the secrets in every human heart, and thus He is qualified to act as your Judge.[20] It is as if God has a video camera secretly recording the evidence of human corruption.

159

At the Marketplace: The Weigh Scale Tells All

As an anonymous American economist shared with me (a lowly weigh scale, think of it!) recently: "You can trick the customer, but you can't trick God. In fact, God is the third party to the transaction."

Sometimes, I am jealous of those rare weigh scales whose owners are honest and transparent. Perhaps that's because, as Proverbs 16:11 states, their true owner, after all, is God: "A just balance and scales are the Lord's."

And since the Bible also says that He "loves" honest weight scales, "Does anyone have His phone number?!"

SUMMARY

1. Corruption in the marketplace:
   a. Often involves:
      i. Fraud (stealing paired with deception).
      ii. Collusion (businesses fix prices rather than compete).
      iii. Embezzlement (employees steal from employers).
      iv. Shoplifting (employees and customers steal goods or services).
   b. Dishonest weigh scales:
      i. Are forbidden, because they violate God's character.
      ii. Deserve God's judgment.
   c. To one extent or another, business corruption involves breaking the Eighth, Ninth and Tenth commandments.
2. Bribery and corruption diminish economies by:
   a. Diverting funds away from normal economic activity that promotes economic growth.
   b. Forcing people to underground economies where contracts cannot be enforced.
   c. Reduces the willingness to take financial risks necessary to starting businesses.
   d. Reduces the quality of the private labor force that makes economies thrive.
3. Benefits of an honest economy:

a. Business activity and the economy grow.

b. Those who are honest live longer lives.

4. Public standards can encourage honesty and economic growth through fair distribution policies.

5. Corruption can be conquered if people are willing to lose some personal freedom and rights (as in Singapore).

6. God sees the secrets of every human heart, and judges accordingly, because a "just balance and scales are the Lord's."

STUDY GUIDE

1. Why is honesty in the marketplace and in government essential for a healthy flourishing society?

2. How can you share biblical teaching about honest businesses and marketplaces with businesspeople whom you know?

3. What do you learn about economic development and corruption from the example of Singapore?

4. What practical idea for "Taming the Beast" (found in the Appendix) will you and your group deploy as a result of reading this chapter?

NOTES

1. Amos 8:6. *"That we may buy the poor for silver and the needy for a pair of sandals and sell the chaff of the wheat?"*

2. Leviticus 19:35-36. *"You shall do no wrong in judgment, in measures of length or weight or quantity. You shall have just balances, just weights, a just ephah, and a just hin: I am the LORD your God, who brought you out of the land of Egypt."* Proverbs 20:10. *Unequal weights and unequal measures are both alike an abomination to the Lord.* Proverbs 20:23. *Unequal weights are an abomination to the Lord, and false scales are not good.*

3. Deuteronomy 25:13-16. *"You shall not have in your bag two kinds of weights, a large and a small. You shall not have in your house two kinds of measures, a large and a small. A full and fair weight you shall have, a full*

161

and fair measure you shall have, that your days may be long in the land that the LORD your God is giving you. For all who do such things, all who act dishonestly, are an abomination to the LORD your God."

4. See also Proverbs 20:10, 23.

5. Micah 6:11. *Shall I acquit the man with wicked scales and with a bag of deceitful weights?*

6. Leviticus 19:13. *"You shall not oppress your neighbor or rob him. The wages of a hired worker shall not remain with you all night until the morning."*

7. Psalm 50:18. *If you see a thief, you are pleased with him, and you keep company with adulterers.* Proverbs. 29:24. *The partner of a thief hates his own life; he hears the curse, but discloses nothing.*[s]

8. Chris E. McGoey, *Shoplifting Facts: Retail Theft of Merchandise.* Downloaded February 2, 2016 from http://www.crimedoctor.com/shoplifting-facts.htm.

9. Amos 8:4-6. *Hear this, you who trample on the needy and bring the poor of the land to an end, saying, "When will the new moon be over, that we may sell grain. And the Sabbath, that we may offer wheat for sale, that we may make the ephah small and the shekel great and deal deceitfully with false balances, that we may buy the poor for silver and the needy for a pair of sandals and sell the chaff of the wheat?"* Hosea 12:7. *A merchant, in whose hands are false balances, he loves to oppress.*

10. Lipset, S.M. & Lenz, G.S., "Corruption, culture, and markets," p. 112 in L.E. Harrison & S.P. Huntington (Eds.), *Culture matters: How values shape human progress* (New York: Basic Books, 2000), 112-125.

11. Hernando de Soto, *The Mystery of Capital* (New York: Basic Books, 2003).

12. Numbers 30:1-2. *Moses spoke to the heads of the tribes of the people of Israel, saying, "This is what the LORD has commanded. If a man vows a vow to the LORD, or swears an oath to bind himself by a pledge, he shall not*

break his word. He shall do according to all that proceeds out of his mouth."
Acts 5:1-10. *But a man named Ananias, with his wife Sapphira, sold a piece of property, and with his wife's knowledge he kept back for himself some of the proceeds and brought only a part of it and laid it at the apostles' feet. But Peter said, "Ananias, why has Satan filled your heart to lie to the Holy Spirit and to keep back for yourself part of the proceeds of the land? While it remained unsold, did it not remain your own? And after it was sold, was it not at your disposal? Why is it that you have contrived this deed in your heart? You have not lied to man but to God." When Ananias heard these words, he fell down and breathed his last. And great fear came upon all who heard of it. The young men rose and wrapped him up and carried him out and buried him. After an interval of about three hours his wife came in, not knowing what had happened. And Peter said to her, "Tell me whether you sold the land for so much." And she said, "Yes, for so much." But Peter said to her, "How is it that you have agreed together to test the Spirit of the Lord? Behold, the feet of those who have buried your husband are at the door, and they will carry you out." Immediately she fell down at his feet and breathed her last. When the young men came in they found her dead, and they carried her out and buried her beside her husband.* I John 2:5. *Wbut whoever keeps his word, in him truly the love of God is perfected. By this we may know that we are in him.*

13. Numbers 23:19. *God is not man, that he should lie, or a son of man, that he should change his mind. Has he said, and will he not do it? Or has he spoken, and will he not fulfill it?* Proverbs 28:13. *Whoever conceals his transgressions will not prosper, but he who confesses and forsakes them will obtain mercy.* Ephesians 4:15. *Rather, speaking the truth in love, we are to grow up in every way into him who is the head, into Christ.* Ephesians 4:25. *Therefore, having put away falsehood, let each one of you speak the truth with his neighbor, for we are members one of another.*

14. Deuteronomy 25:15. *A full and fair weight you shall have, a full and fair measure you shall have, that your days may be long in the land that the LORD your God is giving you.*

15. Genesis 1:26-27. *Then God said, "Let us make man in our image, after our likeness. And let them have dominion over the fish of the sea and over the birds of the heavens and over the livestock and over all the earth and over*

every creeping thing that creeps on the earth." So God created man in his own image, in the image of God he created him; male and female he created them.

16. cf. Numbers 33 and Joshua 13. Joshua 18:6. *And you shall describe the land in seven divisions and bring the description here to me. And I will cast lots for you here before the LORD our God.*

17. Proverbs 22:28. *Do not move the ancient landmark that your fathers have set.* Proverbs 23:10. *Do not move an ancient landmark or enter the fields of the fatherless.*

18. Joshua 14:14. *Therefore Hebron became the inheritance of Caleb the son of Jephunneh the Kenizzite to this day, because he wholly followed the LORD, the God of Israel.*

19. Joshua 19:49. *This is the inheritance of the tribe of the people of Dan, according to their clans—these cities with their villages.*

20. Jeremiah 17:10. *"I the LORD search the heart and test the mind, to give every man according to his ways, according to the fruit of his deeds."* Isaiah 33:22. *For the LORD is our judge; the LORD is our lawgiver; the LORD is our king; he will save us.* Isaiah 44:21. *Remember these things, O Jacob, and Israel, for you are my servant; I formed you; you are my servant; O Israel, you will not be forgotten by me.* I Corinthians 2:11. *For who knows a person's thoughts except the spirit of that person, which is in him? So also no one comprehends the thoughts of God except the Spirit of God.*

CHAPTER TEN

A Confession from the Teacher's Desk

"How do we teach integrity in a world filled with corruption?"

Every teacher has a desk. Well, almost every teacher. Surprisingly, we hear nothing about a desk or anything like it in the story of Jesus.

In this tale, our desk—which could be located in any one of over 10 million classrooms around the world—is a confessor. The desk, brought to life in this narrative, has stories to tell, just like the mouse, the weigh scale, and all the other witnesses to the universe of corruption.

Think about what happens at teachers' desks: People pound them in frustration, but, more often, students go there cooperatively at the teacher's summons. It is also where grades are assigned, and so, in a very real way, a teacher's desk is a judgment seat from which one's future is determined

A Confession from the Teacher's Desk

(especially if a student aspires to a leading university).

The teacher's desk has a confession, a tell-all tale, and that is what this chapter is about. This desk knows what many teachers may try to hide from themselves: Integrity, or honesty, is the backbone of education. When students learn that their teacher can't be trusted, or that you can be purchased at a price, their respect for knowledge diminishes, and their society with it.

Now, let's hear from the desk itself...

****

My story begins in an Indonesian factory where I was cut, glued and screwed together to become the lowly teacher's desk that I am. I have had a long life for a teacher's desk, having served in this role for 11 years.

Of course, long life for a desk means serving many thousands of students and more teachers than I can count.

Unfortunately, I haven't seen as many teachers as you might think. You see, a lot of the teachers assigned to my desk (and other desks in my school) show up to teach about once each month. Eager to learn, children throng their classrooms every day, but, alas, their educators are truant.

Except for that one day when they come to pick up their paychecks!

Of course, some teachers show up everyday, or almost. (I've heard there are places in the world where teachers come to class everyday. What dedication!)

Their students have wonderful learning opportunities. They learn how to write in their mother tongue as well as in the language used for commercial business and public affairs. They learn basic mathematics, as well as science. And, most certainly, they learn about how to behave morally, much of it by observing their teachers' behaviors.

Now, what do you suppose the students learn from teachers who rarely show up in the classroom (except to collect their paychecks) or who show little interest in their students? These teachers are guilty of fraud: stealing instructional hours from their students while also collecting paychecks from the government. Fraud is one of the many forms of corruption. Will their students learn the moral lessons and skills necessary for taming the beast of corruption?

My underlying question is this: How can a teacher instruct students to be honest in a corrupt society when they are actively complicit in the corruption by failing to teach (or, by hiring someone less qualified to teach in their place)? Even if they are personally corrupt, most teachers and parents don't want children to be corrupt. They want to them to be good, no doubt because God has built his moral law inside of them, just as he has in every human being.[1] But, how will they succeed, if they are corrupt themselves?

However, teaching integrity in a classroom is much harder than you might imagine. Perhaps this is because honesty is partially developed through making good and wise choices, and children have relatively few opportunities for that. Often, they are simply expected to repeat by rote what the teacher instructs them, never learning *why* integrity is so important in a world filled with corruption.

As places to learn honesty, classrooms do have certain limitations. Those could be overcome if teachers utilized more interesting methods that engage students in learning and making decisions. Imagine what would happen if teachers genuinely engaged their students in the study of profound moral parables.

The truth is that most humans learn morality at home or in the community. A great deal of what children learn comes from observing the lives of people they respect, starting with their parents and then extending to community leaders and teachers. When parents and teachers model corrupt behavior, even though they teach moral behavior, students take note of the hypocrisy. In most cases, lacking compelling examples of honesty, the students will themselves become corrupt like the rest of their societies.

Teaching integrity *is* hard…

(The chattering noises of eager children suddenly fill the classroom. Will the instructor also enter to teach the students?)

I need to finish this later in the evening after the children have left school…

****

A Confession from the Teacher's Desk

…Good evening! It was a long day, but finally, around 11 am, the instructor showed up, and the children actually learned some useful knowledge.

Obstacles to Teaching Integrity

Where were we? Oh, yes… Formal moral instruction in the classroom is hard. Most people learn their morality at home or in their community where they observe the moral lives of those they respect.

Another reason why teaching integrity is hard is because corruption is like a beast that insists on reproducing itself in the young, entrapping its victims with its claws. As you learned already in the tale of the purse (Chapter Two), every human being is fundamentally corrupt. Having observed thousands of children over more than decade, I doubt that many of them realize how strongly they are lured to corrupt, dishonest ways. Unless people are loyal to Jesus Christ, the desires of the human heart are overpowered by the evil that surrounds and is in them.

The great Jewish leader Moses, who led the Jewish people to escape from Egyptian captivity, twice warned them that after his death they would become corrupt.[2] The Book of Judges tells the sad story: They "returned to ways even more corrupt than their fathers," time after time.[3] Their passion for idols, the things they become devoted to in place of the True God who created everything, epitomized their corruption (see Chapter Seven).

The temptation to idolatry within each human being is best exemplified by greed, and that fuels corruption (see Chapter Six). King Solomon's decline as a leader began when he became incredibly wealthy,[4] He was wealthier than any other leader on the earth, so much so that he was able to generate an annual income equal to almost $1.5 billion. With that kind of wealth, he could support at least 1000 wives and concubines.

Did Solomon's enormous material successes breed the conditions under which his sons became foolishly corrupt?[5]

While the tentacles of corruption are everywhere, there *are*, nevertheless, good answers to the question, "How can children be taught integrity in the midst of dishonest and corrupt societies?" Let me suggest a few.

Tell Stories about Honesty

A teacher can start by telling stories that capture the imagination while also promoting honesty. A wise teacher—and I have seen a few of them over my many years as a desk—will survey and ponder the moral stories that are told within the society, and will then focus on the ones that teach integrity. Americans, for example, have a story they tell about what one of their presidents, Abraham Lincoln. The story is told that when he was a very young shopkeeper, he received one penny too much from a customer, and when he later realized the mistake, he ran after the customer to return their penny. Told properly, that story captures the child's imagination for honesty.

At a gathering of emerging young intellectuals from his continent, one young African leader considered the moral impact of the stories parents tell their children. He reminded them that in their world parents and elders tells stories about tigers and other animals that sneak up behind people to take advantage of them. These "trickster" stories fuel sneaky, corrupt behavior in impressionable children. By contrast, Chinese children learn that they have a responsibility to develop themselves morally. Their emphasis on moral education, however, is often undercut when students learn that their moral heroes are also corrupt. Moral hypocrisy not only sabotages moral education, but it weakens your capacity to tame the beast of corruption.

Consider the story of the prophet Elisha who healed the foreign leader Naaman. Embedded in this fascinating narrative is a lesson about honesty. Though he was a gifted Aramean military leader, Naaman was afflicted with leprosy. Thanks to a young Hebrew servant who told his wife about a Jewish prophet and healer named Elisha, he showed up at Elisha's door in search of a healing potion. Flabbergasted that Elisha merely wanted him to dip himself in the River Jordan, only because his advisors coaxed him did Naaman do as Elisha had told him. Miraculously, he was healed, and, to express his thanks, he brought a load of gifts to Elisha. But, Elisha was a man completely above reproach, and lest he use his miraculous gift to become personally wealthy, he refused the gifts. But, his assistant Gehazi was a man who not only sought the gifts that Elisha refused, but then he lied about getting them from Naaman. As a result, Gehazi ended up with the same disease from which Naaman was cured![6]

Any small child who hears this story will learn that coveting and lying (elements at the core of corruption) can be personally harmful.

Good teachers teach stories about honesty that catch the child's imagination.

Teach Integrity to Parents

Teaching the children's parents such stories is another way to teach integrity. Parents need to learn that honesty is important for the future of their community. A dedicated teacher has the respect of parents, and they will listen to the teacher. Children can be given assignments incorporating the theme of integrity, and asked to complete them with their parents' assistance. In doing so, parents "teach" their children. Teachers can also organize annual community seminars to instruct parents that honesty is important for students' academic successes, but also essential for the future health of the community and the nation.

But, there are enormous challenges built into this effort. It should be remembered that even if you teach integrity to children and their parents, when individuals get on with life or even attain a position of power (as when someone becomes a politician), they may be drawn to corruption, especially if it is already a norm in the society. Abraham was surrounded by corruption in Sodom and Gomorrah, but God firmly commanded him to "command his children and his household after him to keep the way of the Lord by doing righteousness and justice."[7] Because the lure of corruption is a great fear of godly people around the world, parents should be coached to train their children to learn at an early age to resist evil. Many parents are not afraid to subject their children to rigorous academic and sports training; why not also subject them to rigorous moral training as well?

What do you think? Remember, I am merely a desk. You humans are the ones who must train your children to be honest and to resist the moral impurity and corruption of the surrounding society.

A wise teacher, knowing the immensity of the challenge, will coach parents so they can guide their children to put themselves under the sovereign power of the God of the Universe, knowing that He is just and expects us to live righteous lives as well.

Model Integrity

Not only should the teacher help parents understand the importance of integrity, but teachers have tremendous opportunities to model integrity to their students. As the saying goes, "More is caught than taught," which means that one's virtuous example "speaks volumes" to attentive students.

The greatest of the Jewish kings, David, demonstrated remarkable integrity and wisdom by storing up the necessary supplies (which included gold, silver, and bronze) that his son Solomon would later use when building the Temple, which functioned as a major public facility in Israel.[8] Tragically, many of today's leaders would steal these same supplies for themselves, never thinking to save anything for their successors.

David, however, went beyond wise and honest stewardship of public funds. He also gave from his personal treasury! "Moreover, in addition to all that I have provided for the holy house, I have a treasure of my own of gold and silver, and because of my devotion to the house of God I give it to the house of my God" (I Chronicles 29:3). What public leader today would give his personal funds for public purposes?!

As a result of David's personal generosity, the people rejoiced: "And whoever had precious stones gave them to the treasury of the house of the Lord, in the care of Jehiel the Gershonite, Then the people rejoiced because they had given willingly, for with a whole heart they had offered freely to the Lord. David also rejoiced."[9] David combined honesty with generosity, and the populace followed his example.

The Temple, built in approximately 1100 BC, was a public facility. In our time, this would be the equivalent of giving money for the building of the national parliament.

In fact, honest people can afford to be generous, both because integrity is often rewarded with financial success (in societies that reward, instead of punish integrity) and because their faith in God drives them to seek higher priorities than accumulating wealth for themselves.[10]

Teachers, as well as parents, government officials, and businesspeople, must model integrity, both by their diligence as teachers, but also by talking openly about resisting temptations to personal corruption, with the power of God.

Storytelling about and modeling integrity, combined with special instruction to parents about the importance of integrity, are three critical ways that teachers can teach honesty. But, teachers, by virtue of their role as instructors in the community, should also publicly advocate holding people accountable to a standard of integrity even as they also teach that standard.

Teach and Advocate for Public Accountability

God holds everyone accountable.[11] When a person is corrupt in the exercise of their duties, they must suffer negative consequences, either now or later.

But, many officials and powerful people are never held accountable for their crimes of corruption because the law is not respected. In other societies the powerful can buy their way out of punishment for their crimes, unlike the poor and defenseless. Because the corrupt are not punished, corruption becomes more widespread.

Societies that respect the rule of law are, first of all, societies that have learned to respect God's rule. Teachers and preachers must inculcate respect for a God who sees what you think and do in secret, and who holds you accountable for that (either by way of judgment or reward).[12]

Having taught that each person is accountable to God, teachers can then join with other community leaders and advocate for public accountability, explaining to their children reasons why public accountability is essential to the long-term effort to decrease corruption (see Chapter Eight).

There is yet a fourth strategy that teachers can undertake in order to cultivate a love for honesty, which, in turn, will undermine cultures of corruption. Teachers must confront false ideas about truth that pervade most societies and which directly contribute to corruption.

Teach a Proper View of Truth

When it comes to its absolute commitment to the truth, referring to the "fit" between reality and what we say it is, Christianity is unique among the world's religions. If I say that a tree is made of gold, then I evaluate that statement by asking: "Is it true?" If the claim does not match the reality, then we can easily see that I am not telling the truth. Because of this high commitment to truth, humans are frustrated by leaders and societies that tolerate corruption even while also claiming to be Christians.

In many societies, truth is seen as whatever works. If a statement achieves a desirable goal, then it is accepted as truth. Suppose a teacher tells an education administrator that he has collected US$100 from his students as payment for school uniforms (when, in reality, he has actually collected US$200). If the official gives him the uniforms, then he is satisfied that he has told them the "truth." Why? Because his statement achieved the goal, which was to get the uniforms for the children. As you can see, this idea of truth opens the door to massive corruption.

Another faulty concept of truth is that it is determined by community members' agreement, not whether it actually fits with reality. No human can deny that her friends, her close associates, and her community help shape her idea of what is true. Humans all share the problem by virtue of the fact that they are sinners and because they are finite.

But, my concern is different: Many times in some multi-ethnic societies people are forbidden to contradict the claims made by members of their own ethnic or religious group, even when those claims contradict the facts (as best they can determine them). This leads to massive corruption, because cheating people from other ethnic groups is very easily justified if truth is only what your group claims it to be. Is this why some Muslims, for example, have a special teaching that allows them to tell lies in order to further advance the cause of Islam?[13] And could this, in turn, be why some historically Islamic societies have a very high rate of corruption, according to Transparency International data (see Chapter Eleven)?

Societies with the Bible's high view of truth (where claims must match reality) encourage human flourishing, while those that reject this view have a higher probability of widespread poverty. This claim can generally be confirmed by consulting evidence regarding the Gross Domestic Product per capita in each nation.[14]

When the Bible says to "keep corrupt talk from your lips," it means that lies are forbidden because they are inherently destructive and promoted by "scoundrels and villains."[15] Those who are committed to speaking truth are even willing to suffer loss, which is what happened to the prophet Balaam whom Balak tried to pay off so that he would utter lies.[16]

Wise teachers will discuss problematic views of truth with their children, and ensure that the children learn strong arguments for the view that truth must correspond to reality as it really is. Children can be attentive and attracted to truth. This will help them cultivate resistance to the culture of corruption.

Finally, teachers can do one more thing to help train up a new generation that resists the lure of corruption. They must teach that honesty is rewarded.

Teach that Honesty Is Rewarded

The apostle Paul set a powerful example of integrity in the New Testament era when he addressed the elders at Ephesus, "I have not coveted anyone's silver or gold or clothing."[17] But, why was Paul so insistent on not coveting? Because, Paul knew Jesus' words were true: "It is more blessed to give than to receive."[18] So, while the Jewish leaders of His era were known to bribe others, as they did with Judas Iscariot whom they paid 30 pieces of silver, Jesus radically altered the vision of how we are to live: Live generously so as to enrich others.[19]

Teachers should also draw attention to the story of Zacchaeus, a corrupt tax collector who became a follower of Jesus and then paid back four times what he stole through corrupt activities.[20] He perfectly illustrates what a corrupt person should do when he becomes right with God: provide restitution to those from whom he stole.

174

Teachers can offer examples from their own lives that demonstrate that honesty has its own rewards. Teachers can offer their students tangible rewards for honesty, provided they explain that such rewards are meant to build good moral habits and not because all virtue has such pleasant rewards. As always, pointing children to biblical illustrations of integrity is critical.

As I have demonstrated, effective teaching that breaks the culture of corruption must incorporate six elements: 1) modeling integrity; 2) storytelling about honesty; 3) teaching parents why honesty is so important; 4) teaching and advocating that people must be held accountable when they lack integrity; 5) teaching students a proper view of truth; and 6) teaching that honesty is rewarded.

There are, however, real and significant challenges to teaching integrity, especially in our secular era.

Challenges to Teaching Integrity in a Secular Era

King David's example, as recorded in I Chronicles 29, stuns people in our modern era. The reason why such integrity and generosity is so rare today is that our modern nation-states are secular. That is, they function independent of God the Lawgiver who shows mercy and shares His grace while also punishing those who break His law. Our secular nations expect people to be honest without reference to a divine lawgiver. By contrast, the Jews of David's era were not only profoundly inspired by David's example of integrity,[21] but their entire society was built around God's Law.

King David clearly understood that God was the source of his power and wealth, and thus his generosity and integrity were built upon a foundation that was God-centered: "But who am I, and what is my people, that we should be able thus to offer willingly? For all things come from you, and of your own have we given you...O Lord our God, all this abundance that we have provided for building you a house for your holy name comes from your hand and is all your own."[22]

Though governments today hire teachers and admonish them to be honest, government leaders often undercut the message of integrity when they use public funds for themselves. And, unfortunately, teachers are frequently not allowed to point students to God as the original lawgiver.[23] In effect the students are left with no adequate models of integrity.

Special Challenges for Those Who Study in the West

Those who return from study in the West are positioned for leadership in their home societies, but they have two challenges with respect to the matter of teaching integrity. The first challenge concerns the corrupt expectations that many have for them:

> There are many Africans who, educated in the West and returning home with ideas they have acquired in Europe or America, have been ridiculed, even by their own families, if they choose not to follow what are presented to them as local cultural conventions in matters of political morality. This can involve attitudes to life and death, but perhaps more commonly relates to the combination of public office and personal enrichment known as corruption. 'Former public officials or civil servants who do not have booties to show for their period of service are ridiculed and decried as failures,' writes an expatriate Liberian. 'They are scorned and badmouthed, simply because they failed to do the "cultural thing": to exploit the public coffers.'[24]

As demonstrated in the quote above, international students are often expected to use their advanced education in order to join the corrupt elite back home. This must be resisted at all costs.

The second challenge often arises long before they return home. Many of their Western professors in the humanities (art, literature, history, and philosophy) and the social sciences (economics, education, sociology, political science, social work, and anthropology) teach that truth is a masquerade for power, and that the real goal of education is not to pursue truth, but to correct power imbalances. The late Stanford philosopher Richard Rorty demonstrated this cynicism toward truth when he declared that "truth is what your contemporaries let you get away with." While unjust uses of power is a real problem in most societies, cynicism toward truth undermines the call to cleanse societies of bribery and corruption. Unless they know that God declares it wrong, most people will go along with corruption because it is also fine with members of their immediate community. This cynical view of truth combines the two false views of truth that I described before: truth as what works and truth as what your community determines to be true.

Traditionally, Western higher education was dedicated to the pursuit of truth. Those who studied in the West and returned home were potentially able to contribute to the effort to end corruption. But, now, the hunger to end the culture of corruption in our societies has become harder because Western philosophers and academics dethrone the quest for truth in favor of the quest for power. This bad idea inadvertently fuels corruption.

As a lowly desk, I'm used to being silent, letting others use me as their platform to teach. But, as you can see, I'm angry that the West is undermining your quest for transparency. One thing, however, encourages me: Jesus Christ taught His followers that the pursuit of truth is worth your life. He told them that He would give them the words they need in order to honestly testify to their faith before those who persecute them.[25] Even the Pharisees had to admit, "Teacher, we know that you are true and teach the way of God truthfully, and you do not care about anyone's opinion, for you are not swayed by appearances."[26] Jesus said elsewhere that "you shall know the truth, and the truth shall set you free."[27]

Those who follow Jesus herald truth and should be relentlessly committed to integrity—in their lives, their classrooms, and in their neighborhoods. The best hope for the international students who go to the West from our nations is Jesus Christ, "the way, the truth and the life."[28] They become part of a community—the church—that possesses a "high view of truth." They discover a comprehensive perspective on reality that is often called a "Christian worldview". This perspective works greatly to them make sense of society and culture through the eyes of Jesus Christ.

It is essential that the best-educated in a society embrace a high view of truth. Unless that happens, teachers will have an enormous challenge in instilling in their students the values of honesty and integrity. But, until such students emerge and become leaders in their societies, the destruction and despair of corruption is likely to live on.

From my place here in the teacher's classroom, I can see that the sun is just beginning to peek up from behind the trees. Soon, students and, I hope, their teacher will again fill this classroom with a hunger to learn. Perhaps one of them will help lead the campaign to end corruption.

As a mere desk, that would be more than I could ever ask for!

SUMMARY

1. Obstacles to teaching integrity in the classroom:
    a. Integrity is learned primarily by observing the behavior of those we respect.
    b. Corruption constantly tries to reproduce itself in the young.
2. How to teach integrity to children:
    a. Tell stories about honesty that include:
        i. Stories about respected national leaders.
        ii. Morality tales.
        iii. Biblical stories of integrity.
    b. Teach integrity to parents.
    c. Model integrity.
    d. Teach and advocate for public accountability.
    e. Teach a proper view of truth.
    f. Teach that honesty has its rewards.
3. Challenges to teaching integrity in a modern era:
    a. Secularism limits our capacities to teach from God's Word in public schools.
    b. Public officials are often the worst possible examples of integrity.
    c. Leaders trained as international students in Western universities:
        i. Are pressured to join the corrupt elite when they return home.
        ii. Often learn a postmodern version of truth that undermines the call to personal and national integrity.

Taming The Beast

STUDY GUIDE

1. Think about someone who influenced you toward either a life of integrity or one of deception. Why were they so effective in your life?
2. What are the challenges in your society that are obstacles against teaching honesty and integrity? How can you and your friends overcome that obstacle?
3. Think of a child whom you hope to influence toward integrity. What will you do (and what biblical texts will you utilize) in order to be successful in your effort?
4. What practical idea for "Taming the Beast" (found in the Appendix) will you and your group deploy as a result of reading this chapter?

NOTES

1. Romans 2:14-15. *For when Gentiles, who do not have the law, by nature do what the law requires, they are a law to themselves, even though they do not have the law. They show that the work of the law is written on their hearts, while their conscience also bears witness, and their conflicting thoughts accuse or even excuse them.*

2. Deuteronomy 31:29. *"For I know that after my death you will surely act corruptly and turn aside from the way that I have commanded you. And in the days to come evil will befall you, because you will do what is evil in the sight of the LORD, provoking him to anger through the work of your hands."* Deuteronomy 32:5. *They have dealt corruptly with him; they are no longer his children because they are blemished; they are a crooked and twisted generation.*

3. Judges 2:19. *But whenever the judge died, they turned back and were more corrupt than their fathers, going after other gods, serving them and bowing down to them. They did not drop any of their practices or their stubborn ways.*

4. I Kings 10:14-29. *Now the weight of gold that came to Solomon in one year was 666 talents of gold, besides that which came from the explorers and from the business of the merchants, and from all the kings of the west and from*

the governors of the land. King Solomon made 200 large shields of beaten gold; 600 shekels of gold went into each shield. And he made 300 shields of beaten gold; three minas of gold went into each shield. And the king put them in the House of the Forest of Lebanon. The king also made a great ivory throne and overlaid it with the finest gold. The throne had six steps, and the throne had a round top, and on each side of the seat were armrests and two lions standing beside the armrests, while twelve lions stood there, one on each end of a step on the six steps. The like of it was never made in any kingdom. All King Solomon's drinking vessels were of gold, and all the vessels of the House of the Forest of Lebanon were of pure gold. None were of silver; silver was not considered as anything in the days of Solomon. For the king had a fleet of ships of Tarshish at sea with the fleet of Hiram. Once every three years the fleet of ships of Tarshish used to come bringing gold, silver, ivory, apes, and peacocks. Thus King Solomon excelled all the kings of the earth in riches and in wisdom. And the whole earth sought the presence of Solomon to hear his wisdom, which God had put into his mind. Every one of them brought his present, articles of silver and gold, garments, myrrh, spices, horses, and mules, so much year by year. And Solomon gathered together chariots and horsemen. He had 1,400 chariots and 12,000 horsemen, whom he stationed in the chariot cities and with the king in Jerusalem. And the king made silver as common in Jerusalem as stone, and he made cedar as plentiful as the sycamore of the Shephelah. And Solomon's import of horses was from Egypt and Kue, and the king's traders received them from Kue at a price. A chariot could be imported from Egypt for 600 shekels of silver and a horse for 150, and so through the king's traders they were exported to all the kings of the Hittites and the kings of Syria.

5. I Kings 11:1-8. *Now King Solomon loved many foreign women, along with the daughter of Pharaoh: Moabite, Ammonite, Edomite, Sidonian, and Hittite women, from the nations concerning which the LORD had said to the people of Israel, "You shall not enter into marriage with them, neither shall they with you, for surely they will turn away your heart after their gods." Solomon clung to these in love. He had 700 wives, who were princesses, and 300 concubines. And his wives turned away his heart. For when Solomon was old his wives turned away his heart after other gods, and his heart was not wholly true to the LORD his God, as was the heart of David his father. For Solomon went after Ashtoreth the goddess of the Sidonians, and after Milcom the abomination of the Ammonites. So Solomon did what was evil in the sight of the LORD and did not wholly follow the LORD, as David his father had done. Then Solomon built a high place for Chemosh the abomination of Moab,*

and for Molech the abomination of the Ammonites, on the mountain east of Jerusalem. And so he did for all his foreign wives, who made offerings and sacrificed to their gods.

6. II Kings 5: 19b-27. *But when Naaman had gone from him a short distance, Gehazi, the servant of Elisha the man of God, said, "See, my master has spared this Naaman the Syrian, in not accepting from his hand what he brought. As the LORD lives, I will run after him and get something from him." So Gehazi followed Naaman. And when Naaman saw someone running after him, he got down from the chariot to meet him and said, "Is all well?" And he said, "All is well. My master has sent me to say, 'There have just now come to me from the hill country of Ephraim two young men of the sons of the prophets. Please give them a talent of silver and two changes of clothing.'" And Naaman said, "Be pleased to accept two talents." And he urged him and tied up two talents of silver in two bags, with two changes of clothing, and laid them on two of his servants. And they carried them before Gehazi. And when he came to the hill, he took them from their hand and put them in the house, and he sent the men away, and they departed. He went in and stood before his master, and Elisha said to him, "Where have you been, Gehazi?" And he said, "Your servant went nowhere." But he said to him, "Did not my heart go when the man turned from his chariot to meet you? Was it a time to accept money and garments, olive orchards and vineyards, sheep and oxen, male servants and female servants? Therefore the leprosy of Naaman shall cling to you and to your descendants forever." So he went out from his presence a leper, like snow.*

7. Genesis 18:19. *"For I have chosen him, that he may command his children and his household after him to keep the way of the LORD by doing righteousness and justice, so that the LORD may bring to Abraham what he has promised him."*

8. I Chronicles 29:1-2. *And David the king said to all the assembly, "Solomon my son, whom alone God has chosen, is young and inexperienced, and the work is great, for the palace will not be for man but for the LORD God. So I have provided for the house of my God, so far as I was able, the gold for the things of gold, the silver for the things of silver, and the bronze for the things of bronze, the iron for the things of iron, and wood for the things of*

wood, besides great quantities of onyx and stones for setting, antimony, colored stones, all sorts of precious stones and marble."

9. I Chronicles 29:8-9. *And whoever had precious stones gave them to the treasury of the house of the LORD, in the care of Jehiel the Gershonite. Then the people rejoiced because they had given willingly, for with a whole heart they had offered freely to the LORD. David the king also rejoiced greatly.*

10. Matthew 6:19-21. *"Do not lay up for yourselves treasures on earth, where moth and rust destroy and where thieves break in and steal, but lay up for yourselves treasures in heaven, where neither moth nor rust destroys and where thieves do not break in and steal. For where your treasure is, there your heart will be also."*

11. Psalm 73:27. *"For behold, those who are far from you shall perish; you put an end to everyone who is unfaithful to you."* Romans 14:12. *"So then each of us will give an account of himself to God."*

12. Matthew 6:2-6. *"Thus, when you give to the needy, sound no trumpet before you, as the hypocrites do in the synagogues and in the streets, that they may be praised by others. Truly, I say to you, they have received their reward. But when you give to the needy, do not let your left hand know what your right hand is doing, so that your giving may be in secret. And your Father who sees in secret will reward you. "And when you pray, you must not be like the hypocrites. For they love to stand and pray in the synagogues and at the street corners, that they may be seen by others. Truly, I say to you, they have received their reward. But when you pray, go into your room and shut the door and pray to your Father who is in secret. And your Father who sees in secret will reward you."*

13. This is called *taqiyyah*.

14. cf. Sarah Biddle's work: -
https://commons.wikimedia.org/wiki/File:GDP_per_capita_(no
minal)_2014.png#/media/File:GDP_per_capita_(nominal)_2014.
png.

15. Proverbs 4:24. *Put away from you crooked speech, and put devious talk far from you.* cf. Proverbs 6:12. *A worthless person, a wicked man, goes about with crooked speech.*

16. Numbers 24:13. *Balak should give me his house full of silver and gold, I would not be able to go beyond the word of the LORD, to do either good or bad of my own will. What the LORD speaks, that will I speak'?*

17. Acts 20:33. *"I coveted no one's silver or gold or apparel."*

18. Acts 20:35. *"In all things I have shown you that by working hard in this way we must help the weak and remember the words of the Lord Jesus, how he himself said, 'It is more blessed to give than to receive.'"*

19. II Corinthians 8:9. *For you know the grace of our Lord Jesus Christ, that though he was rich, yet for your sake he became poor, so that you by his poverty might become rich.*

20. Luke 19:1-9. *He entered Jericho and was passing through. And behold, there was a man named Zacchaeus. He was a chief tax collector and was rich. And he was seeking to see who Jesus was, but on account of the crowd he could not, because he was small in stature. So he ran on ahead and climbed up into a sycamore tree to see him, for he was about to pass that way. And when Jesus came to the place, he looked up and said to him, "Zacchaeus, hurry and come down, for I must stay at your house today." So he hurried and came down and received him joyfully. And when they saw it, they all grumbled, "He has gone in to be the guest of a man who is a sinner." And Zacchaeus stood and said to the Lord, "Behold, Lord, the half of my goods I give to the poor. And if I have defrauded anyone of anything, I restore it fourfold." And Jesus said to him, "Today salvation has come to this house, since he also is a son of Abraham."*

21. Psalm 78:72. *With upright heart he shepherded them and guided them with his skillful hand.*

22. I Chronicles 29: 14,16. *"But who am I, and what is my people, that we should be able thus to offer willingly? For all things come from you, and of your own have we given you."* I Chronicles 29: 16. *O Lord our God, all*

this abundance that we have provided for building you a house for your holy name comes from your hand and is all your own.

23. The reason that secular Western governments have relatively little problem with this is because the cultural memory of most of their societies is still deeply informed by Christianity.

24. Stephen Ellis and Gerrie Ter Haar, *Worlds of Power: Religious Thought and Political Practice in Africa* (New York: Oxford University Press, 2004), 157.

25. Luke 21:12-15. *But before all this they will lay their hands on you and persecute you, delivering you up to the synagogues and prisons, and you will be brought before kings and governors for my name's sake. This will be your opportunity to bear witness. Settle it therefore in your minds not to meditate beforehand how to answer, for I will give you a mouth and wisdom, which none of your adversaries will be able to withstand or contradict.*

26. Matthew 22:15-16. *Then the Pharisees went and plotted how to entangle him in his words. And they sent their disciples to him, along with the Herodians, saying, "Teacher, we know that you are true and teach the way of God truthfully, and you do not care about anyone's opinion, for you are not swayed by appearances."*

27. John 8:32. *And you will know the truth, and the truth will set you free.*

28. *Jesus said to him, "I am the way, and the truth, and the life. No one comes to the Father except through me."*

CHAPTER ELEVEN

Corruption in the Church: Interview with a Bible Commentary

"How can churches end the corruption within and promote virtuous societies where everyone flourishes?"

Corruption in the Church

Most pastors around the world know that their words and actions as shepherds of their flocks are transparent to the God that has called them to care for their flocks. As both creator and sustainer of the universe, God sees, hears, and knows all our thoughts, words, and actions.[1]

The sacrifice, compassion, wisdom, and heroic leadership of hundreds of thousands of pastors around the world has been compromised, however. Some pastors, especially those who crave visible successes like large congregations, big buildings, or many staff members, engage in immorality and corruption.

In societies full of corruption, many ask how churches can play a major role in diminishing corruption. Unfortunately, we must first ask, "Why are some churches complicit in corruption, and what can be done about the problem?"

To find answers, we conducted another interview, this time with a large Bible commentary that sits in the office of an unnamed pastor in an unidentified nation. Even in an era when most pastors use online aids for Bible study and sermon preparation, they, nevertheless, stock their bookshelves with print books that help them understand the Bible.

Our commentary has an unusual capacity, never before seen on our planet, for communicating like a person. The commentary also has remarkable skills of observation, not only observing corruption in his church, but having also collected evidence about corruption in other churches worldwide. Because he does his job so well, he also has discovered how the church can become a major and successful player in the fight against corruption and the promotion of human flourishing in societies around the world. In short, this is an interview about "vice and virtue" in the church, at least as it relates to corruption.

Our interview, of course, involved sensitive matters, and so we arranged to meet the commentary in the pastor's office very late one night.

****

I've heard so much about you since you were discovered several years ago by a brilliant undercover investigator whom I respect.

I love serving God, and so I am delighted to share my observations and the evidence I have collected about church corruption *and* indications that churches are becoming centers for promoting virtue instead of vice.

Let's start by hearing about some of the discoveries you

made as you collected evidence about church vice and virtue from around the globe.

The first source I consulted was, of course, Transparency International's *Corruption Perceptions Index* (CPI).[2] Since all truth is God's truth, we can learn from other sources, even secular ones like Transparency International.

The 2015 index contains some stunning data. First, out of 167 nations, nine out of the ten least corrupt nations have an historic Protestant Christian heritage.[3] Their average score is about 86, on a scale where 100 means absolutely free of all corruption and 0 indicates an excessively and overwhelmingly corrupt society. Second, of the ten most corrupt countries, five are historically Islamic.[4] The average score of those five is about 13. This stunning contrast between historically Protestant nations and those with an Islamic heritage powerfully suggests that religion has something to do with the level of corruption in a society.

Two American scholars suggest why historically Protestant societies have rather low levels of corruption: "They (Protestant churches) encourage adherents to press hard to attain and institutionalize virtue and to reduce, if not destroy, the influence of evil people and wicked institutions and practices."[5]

So, we must ask why, in light of the evidence revealed by the CPI, corruption *in* the church worldwide amounts to at least US$3 billion.[6] Christian leaders ought to be very humble about attacking corruption, when, in fact, it has invaded many of our pulpits.

That stings, doesn't it?! If corruption is in many of our churches, then what does that say about our capacity to address this monstrous problem in the larger society?

Paul Gifford, in his book *African Christianity: Its Public Role* (1998), has admonished churches for failing to speak out against corruption, but on what basis could they make a difference? Stephen Ellis and Gerrie Ter Haar warned, rather shockingly, that we should assume many African pastors are corrupt:

Leaders of the latest generation of independent churches,

including those of a charismatic variety, are sometimes regarded as particularly susceptible to lending their support to regimes considered unsavory in liberal quarters.[7]

So, the news is both good and bad. Since, as a Bible commentary, you have privileged access to the Bible's teaching about corruption, what does it say about corruption in the church?

The Bible teaches that all followers of Christ, whether pastors or laypeople, must live virtuous, non-corrupt lives. I Thessalonians 5:22 advises believers to "avoid all appearance of evil." Early Christians had no choice but to be honest and virtuous. Why? Because to live otherwise would have been an utter contradiction of the absolute righteousness of Christ that they claimed was theirs by faith in Him.[8] Jesus' life had been thoroughly virtuous, and so was the expectation concerning theirs.

Furthermore, two New Testament passages, both written to church leaders, reinforce the teaching that, in order to be selected for leadership, a leader must be "completely above reproach."[9] With regard to the way he handled a gift from one church to another, the Apostle Paul wrote that "we want to avoid any criticism of the way we administer this liberal gift...We are taking pains to do what is right, not only in the eyes of the Lord but also in the eyes of men."[10] Personal transparency is an absolute requirement for those who aspire to church leadership because laypeople should have virtuous role models[11].

This was a concern in the Old Testament as well. Before the prophet Samuel died, he asked the Jewish people whether he had extorted them or asked for bribes. He asked because his legacy was at stake. His integrity was a declaration that he loved something greater than himself: He told the truth, even when it was inconvenient and even when it cost him something. He steered clear of luxury, expensive clothes, self-serving handouts, and nepotism. Had he embraced a non-transparent lifestyle, the Jewish people would have cursed rather than blessed him[12].

Leaders, in the church and outside it, have tremendous influence, don't they?

Leaders need to ask themselves: What kind of legacy do you want? When Daniel's enemies tried to harm him, "they could find no corruption in him, because he was trustworthy and neither corrupt nor negligent."[13] Joseph, who resisted the lure of sex with another man's wife,[14] also resisted the lure of corruption while in office as the second most powerful person in all of Egypt. Joshua, Moses' successor, was commanded by God to completely devote himself to God's law was so that he would become the virtuous leader the Jews were willing to follow as they fought for the Promised Land.[15] Nehemiah, another leader like Joshua, courageously rebuilt the walls of Jerusalem after the Jews' exile in Babylon (586-537 BC). Also tasked with instilling courage in his followers, he established a reputation for integrity and refused to take advantage of the people, as had others before him.[16]

Not only do laypeople and Christian leaders need personal transparency, but what is also needed in the church is a culture of transparency. This includes transparency about church finances, methods of operation, constitutions and by-laws, leadership selection, and the decision-making power of congregations.

It's very interesting that you raise this issue. From your perch as a Bible commentary sitting on the pastor's bookshelf, you must have plenty of opportunities to observe the way the church is managed from the pastor's office. Many people would say that the church can run its own business, and nobody needs to know how. So, the question is: Why is transparency in the church essential?

First, Jesus was highly transparent about his mission: "I have spoken openly to the world," Jesus replied. "I always taught in synagogues or at the temple, where all the Jews come together. I said nothing in secret."[17] He had no secrets. He hid nothing from the authorities, both Jewish and Roman. Transparent finances will accompany a transparent mission, whereas an obscured mission conducted in secret opens the door to corrupt and obscure finances. The only reason for non-transparency is when doing so puts others' lives in danger. Consider the wisdom in Jesus' statement: "I am sending you out like sheep among wolves.

Therefore be as shrewd as snakes and as innocent as doves."[18]

A second reason for transparency in the church is the fact that Christianity is hinged on truth. In other words, Christianity not only claims to be built around One who embodied truth,[19] but the text itself advises readers to abandon the faith if its claims are not historical and believable.[20] Living in the darkness is antithetical to the very essence of the faith.[21] Thus, the Apostle Paul writes to the Corinthian believers, "We have renounced secret and shameful ways; we do not use deception, nor do we distort the word of God. On the contrary, by setting forth the truth plainly we commend ourselves to every man's conscience in the sight of God."[22] This example is a strong argument for transparency in others.

Pastoral leaders and their churches have tremendous potential to help tame the beast called corruption. They speak with the voice of God, both in terms of blessing and in terms of judgment. In many countries, they lead the only institution that people respect, and thus their leaders have influence. They have the power to discipline and even ex-communicate those who bring dishonor to Christ.[23] They have significant capacities to educate people.[24] The church is designed to be a model nation that shows the nations and political authorities of the world how to organize their affairs so that humans receive justice and become flourishing.[25] Pastors should not take this responsibility lightly!

That's why corruption in the church is so destructive, isn't it?

We don't really know the extent of corruption in the global church, but it doesn't take much to damage the reputation of Christ's church and to render it ineffective in the battle to tame the beast of corruption. In one recent study, only 20% of the South Korean people trust the leadership of their Protestant churches.[26] In another country, the founder of an evangelical Protestant denomination is considered a collaborator with the highly corrupt regime that dominates his country.

If corruption is tolerated within the church, how can anyone imagine that corruption in government will end? So, the question is: "What will we do about corruption in the church?" Paul wrote believers in Corinth: "But now I am writing you that you must not associate with anyone who calls himself a brother but is sexually immoral or greedy, an idolater or a slanderer, a drunkard or a swindler. With such a man do not even eat...'Purge the evil person from among you.'"[27] Unfortunately, many churches don't take action against flagrant sin. Others welcome people who have been expelled by other churches for these overt sins.

Pope Francis was chosen Pope of the Roman Catholic Church in 2013, in part because of the intense corruption that exists in the curia, that is, the bureaucracy within the Vatican. He knows that the net effect of corruption in the church is that it weakens the personal and corporate integrity of Christ's followers and the institution itself.[28]

So, why do churches tolerate corruption? Don't members feel shame and sorrow, for example, when the leadership of Singapore's largest church was convicted of massive corruption involving US$35 million that was used to support the singing career of the pastor's wife?[29]

I'm sure they do. But, there are at least four reasons why churches tolerate corruption. First of all, pastors in many churches choose not to preach against bribery and corruption because some of their largest contributors are active in bribery and corruption, whether in business or government. When pastoral or denominational leaders are given government positions or receive special government favors, their participation in government often inhibits them from speaking as prophets against corruption.

Secondly, corruption may be tolerated in the church because residual animism still infects the daily lives of members. One writer has suggested that "since animism is built on this foundation of manipulating, bribing and deceiving the spirits, when it comes to dealing with other humans the animist has no convictions against doing the same kinds of things to gain power over others."[30] Could it be that the spirit of animism still influences local churches? Jesus may not be feared and respected as much as neighborhood spirits or the spirits of departed ancestors.

Have church leaders, especially those in Latin America, Africa, and Asia, effectively confronted the false animistic idea that a life-force (blood, human body parts, etc.) must be paid to the spirit world? Much of this involves terribly evil practices that violate biblical morality. One Christian student from Liberia came to study in the USA, where he earned his PhD. Upon his return to Liberia, he entered his nation's senate but was strongly advised in a dream, by friends and his grandfather, to murder someone in order to gain powers to be effective as a politician.[31]

Thirdly, in spite of the fact that many are educated in the USA where corruption is relatively rare, they often go back to their home country and become involved in corruption. In a book about corruption in Kenya, *It's Our Turn to Eat,* author Michaela Wrong cites Kenyan public officials who studied in the USA and who became active members of the corruption clique back in their home country. Another Christian international student who was pursuing a PhD at a leading American university eventually became notorious for the level of corruption in which he was engaged after his return home to Africa. In one celebrated case, the leadership of a major non-Western denomination was taken over by someone who actively collaborated with the leader of the corrupt regime. It is worth noting that this man earned his PhD in an American university.

As suggested in Chapter Ten of this book, one of the reasons some international students engage in corruption back home is because they have embraced a postmodern, cynical perspective on truth that undermines the truth-seeking spirit necessary for conquering corruption. Other Western-educated students may have been seduced by the message of "careerism," namely, that education is about getting a career where you make lots of money. Postmodernism and careerism have diminished the potentially positive effect of Western-educated students. Thought to be natural leaders for the church and broader society, returned students sometimes use their Western education for their own benefit rather than their nation's.

A fourth reason that corruption is tolerated in the church is because some Christian leaders treat their churches as organizations that exist for the enrichment of them and their families. Often, board members and decision makers will reinforce this faulty view of the church by telling such pastors that the church cannot survive without these often dynamic pastors. Have people forgotten that Jesus said, "I will build my church and the gates of hell will not prevail against it?"[32] Christians forfeit their public voice against corruption when they exalt human beings as if they are gods.

Tragically, many churches and their pastoral leaders are implicated in the cultures of corruption in their nations. The prophet Micah gave a terrible indictment against the Jewish nation: "Her elders judge for a bribe, her priests teach for a price, and her prophets tell fortunes for money."[33] All three offices—political leader, pastoral leader, and academic leaders (prophets)—were corrupt. God sees, hears, and knows all the thoughts, words, and actions of human beings.

This is fascinating. What can church leaders do to confront the cancer of corruption within their congregations and denominations?

This is a good question. Let me ask another related, though very sensitive, question: Are Christian leaders, or pastors, willing and ready to make a public accounting of the degree to which corruption and corrupt officials are tolerated in their churches? Church associations within countries around the world must develop "truth commissions" that will research and expose the depth of the problem. Based on the results of the research, churches must hold corrupt pastors and laypeople accountable for their crimes against their fellow citizens and their God.[34] This means that some pastors must be forced to resign their pulpits, and some churches must pursue collective forms of repentance before God. Rather than hiring pastors because they can raise large amounts of money and attract wealthy donors, pastors should be hired according to the degree their practice fits the criteria for church leaders listed in I Timothy 3 and Titus 1.

This extreme action is necessary because the church is expected to take the lead in transforming the culture of corruption. According to Ephesians 3:10, "through the church the manifold wisdom of God (is) made known to the rulers and authorities in the heavenly places." In other words, God's church, by the way it constructs it affairs, by the way it treats its people, by the way it pursues truth, and by the way that it resists corruption, is an example to rulers and authorities who occupy exalted positions of leadership about how to organize their affairs.[35]

In some places, churches are the only recognized and welcome institutions in the society. The church is often the only institution that actively helps the poor and needy in the society. They have the ability to set the moral agenda for the society. In these cases, local government officials often look to the church for examples of how to organize government affairs. Wise political leaders will align themselves with an institution that is seen to be the friend of the people.

Church leaders must not hesitate to speak the whole counsel of God regarding the evil of corruption. They should courageously and eagerly undertake to help their members resist and reform the system by proclaiming week after week the fact that God cannot be bribed (See Chapter One).[36] If God cannot be bribed, then why do human beings, God's image bearers, expect to be bribed?

When Jesus' followers called him "Lord," they used political language only reserved for the Roman ruler Caesar. Because Jesus is Lord, his followers can't avoid the political implications of the Gospel. Other than threats from government leaders, why do some church leaders avoid biblical teaching that refer to the larger social and political realities of their societies? Church leaders simply ought not to shy away from politics.[37] To do so is in some way a denial of Jesus' lordship.

So, the church is in many societies a prominent institution to which others look for guidance and wisdom. Pastors should not be afraid to speak directly from the pulpit about corruption. But, how can church leaders reason with the flocks over which God has made them shepherds?

Church leaders need to teach that corruption is an offense to our basic humanity. Corruption is both a result of the Fall of Adam and Eve into sin and also the cause of much more sin and suffering. Corruption defaces human beings as God's image bearers, and runs counter to every rational thought, moral desire, and social obligation that humans were designed for. Using their

194

minds, humans know that corruption is only rational when one is trying to survive, and they know that it never produces the flourishing that humans desire. Corruption violates every moral norm inside of human beings, and so humans are usually ashamed to be part of it. No one can make a plausible argument that corruption is a moral virtue rather than a vice. Finally, corruption disrupts healthy human relationships, so that the generosity of love is replaced by cold, calculating relationships that depend upon transactions (bribes given and received) in order to keep the relationships functioning.

Pastors must teach that corruption disrupts God's plan for human flourishing, which is the cultural mandate.[38] When people engage in corruption, they have fewer resources—be it time or money—to protect God's creation and to produce those goods and services that help our neighbors flourish. Each of us was designed to contribute to protecting and producing, but corruption helps with neither. Pastors can help their people to see that corruption is not merely a personal matter. It will impact their public lives as workers, as citizens, and as taxpayers, and overtake whatever personal virtue there is in the church. Christians must seek the welfare of the society even if it does not fully appreciate Christ's followers.[39]

Pastors can remind followers of Christ that corruption only belongs in their *past* lives, never in the present.[40] They should teach that corruption violates our dignity as God's image bearers and violates our human purpose as virtuous protectors and producers.[41] Finally, they can show that only through the sinless Son of God, Jesus Christ, is God able to create in each of us a new heart that loves our neighbors, not the vice of corruption.[42]

Many pastors must deal with the generous church donor whose wealth is largely a product of corruption. How will the pastor respond? Almost every pastor will admit that it is very hard to reject such gifts, especially when the pastor and the church desperately need funding. As a way of addressing this need, why couldn't churches elsewhere contribute a fraction of their funds to these pastoral leaders who reject the gifts of the corrupt? They could help save these courageous leaders and their churches from impoverishment. (See Appendix for discussion of proposed

Corruption Amelioration Funds.)

What further temptations must pastors resist?

Pastors must resist three temptations that have taken up residence in some churches. First, some church leaders have embraced what I call a pessimistic "theology of retreat." By this I mean that, rather than teaching that every knee must bow before Jesus,[43] they have embraced the subtly pessimistic message that society's dark, deep sinfulness is beyond the redeeming reach of Jesus. Some suggest a retreat to communities of the faithful, in order to preserve the faith. Some also believe that the Bible teaches we must merely wait for the Rapture, and then all good believers will escape the torment of evil and corruption.

Secondly, many, perhaps most, of our churches have embraced a dualistic worldview that is false, one that prioritizes the spiritual at the expense of the material. This bad idea makes Christianity a private faith designed to satisfy our personal spiritual needs (e.g., forgiveness, healing, finding meaning). While Christian faith does all of these things, dualism tends to weaken the faith of its public power. A truly Christian worldview also teaches that God is concerned about material reality as well as spiritual. God is especially concerned about how we organize our political and economic life. We come back again to that theme: Jesus is Lord of all. As Abraham Kuyper, the Dutch prime minister from 1901-1905, said, "There is not a square inch in the whole domain of our human existence over which Christ, who is Sovereign over all, does not cry, 'Mine!'"

Thirdly, among Western-educated intellectuals, a deep suspicion of human reason and human motivation has short-circuited positive efforts to tame the beast of corruption (see Chapter Ten). As a result of this suspicion of human reason, some pastors have begun to downplay biblical teaching about the authority and trustworthiness of Scripture. Combined with evangelical pessimism, academic postmodernism, and bad theology, there is pressure to avoid confronting the scourge of corruption. More than ever before, our church leaders do well to reread the stories of William Wilberforce and others who, against a great tide of evil that had become institutionalized in the 18th century English church, sought to tame the social beasts of their day, including the slave trade and slavery in the British Empire.[44] And they won ! We can, as well, with God's help.

The world waits for pastors to rise up in the pulpits of their churches and proclaim that corruption has to stop because God simply can't be bribed and neither will He turn a blind eye to evil that destroys people and their societies.

Today, only the church of Jesus Christ and those affiliated with it can point the way out of corruption. Centuries ago, largely Protestant Christian leaders rebuilt their countries, and it can happen again today. It will take courage to remove the cancer of corruption, even those factors, previously mentioned, that cause corruption such as theological pessimism or a dualistic worldview that favors the spiritual over material, or postmodern cynicism, from within churches. Until that happens, the cancer will continue to spread in the larger society.

A remarkable interview. You have thought deeply about this. You are truly a Bible commentary like none other! Thank you.

SUMMARY

1. The least corrupt nations have an historic Protestant Christian heritage, while many of the most corrupt are historically Islamic.
2. Why the church must be transparent and free of corruption.
   a. Laypeople must be transparent, because they possess the perfect righteousness of Christ.
   b. Leaders must be transparent because:
      i. They represent Jesus Christ to the rest of the world.
      ii. They set an example for the church.
      iii. Their legacy has great influence on future generations.
   c. They are a model of a virtuous society to the larger corrupt society.

      i.   Jesus was transparent.

     ii.   Christianity is above all a truth-centered faith.

    iii.   The church is a model nation.

3. Why corruption in the church is a great tragedy
   a. Corruption in the church negates the church's prophetic witness in the larger society.
   b. It weakens the church's internal moral commitments and integrity.

4. Why is corruption tolerated in the church?
   a. Need for wealthy donors.
   b. Residual effect of animism.
   c. Corrosive effect of Western postmodern thought.
   d. Church leaders treat their churches as personal fiefs.

5. How church leaders can confront the cancer of corruption:
   a. Research the nature and degree of church corruption.
   b. Accept the high level of responsibility to be an agenda-setter.
   c. Teach the whole counsel of God, in particular, the fact that corruption diminishes our God-given dignity as well as our capacities to be able protectors and producers (the cultural mandate).
   d. Develop risk-sharing efforts that partially mitigate the effects of resisting corruption.

6. Pastors should also:
   a. Resist a "theology of retreat."
   b. Reject a dualistic approach to Christian faith.
   c. Maintain a high view of their trustworthiness of biblical teaching.

STUDY GUIDE

1. Have you encountered corruption in your church or in other venues with which you are aware? If so:
   a. What has been the response of church leaders?
   b. What was your response upon learning about the corruption?

2. Why has corruption become a problem in some of our churches?
3. What biblical texts would you use to challenge church leaders to face up to corruption within the church?
4. How do you hope the church will tame the beast of corruption in the larger society? How will such efforts bring honor to Jesus Christ?
5. What practical idea for "Taming the Beast" (found in the Appendix) will you and your group employ as a result of reading this chapter?

NOTES

1. Hebrews 4:13; Psalm 33:13; 94:9.

2. The 2013 version employed here is the latest available.

3. Denmark, Netherlands Sweden, Norway, Finland, Switzerland, Australia, New Zealand, and Canada.

4. Sudan, Syria, Turkmenistan, Uzbekistan, Somalia, Libya, Iraq, and Afghanistan.

5. S.M. Lipset & G.S. Lenz, "Corruption, culture, and markets," p. 121. In L.E. Harrison & S.P. Huntington (Eds.), *Culture Matters: How Values Shape Human Progress* (New York: Basic Books, 2000).

6. This estimate was uttered by a respected evangelical leader from Southeast Asia at a November 2012 meeting in Bali, Indonesia.

7. Stephen Ellis and Gerrie Ter Haar, *Worlds of Power: Religious Thought and Political Practice in Africa* (New York: Oxford University Press, 2004), 108

8. Romans 3:22-23. *The righteousness of God through faith in Jesus Christ for all who believe. For there is no distinction: for all have sinned and fall short of the glory of God.* Philippians 3:9. *And be found in him, not having a*

righteousness of my own that comes from the law, but that which comes through faith in Christ, the righteousness from God that depends on faith.

9. I Timothy 3:2. *Therefore an overseer must be above reproach, the husband of one wife, sober-minded, self-controlled, respectable, hospitable, able to teach, not a drunkard, not violent but gentle, not quarrelsome, not a lover of money.* Titus 1:6. *If anyone is above reproach, the husband of one wife, and his children are believers and not open to the charge of debauchery or insubordination.*

10. II Corinthians 8:20-21. *We take this course so that no one should blame us about this generous gift that is being administered by us, for we aim at what is honorable not only in the Lord's sight but also in the sight of man.*

11. I Timothy 4:12. *Let no one despise you for your youth, but set the believers an example in speech, in conduct, in love, in faith, in purity.*

12. I Samuel 12:3-4. *Here I am; testify against me before the LORD and before his anointed. Whose ox have I taken? Or whose donkey have I taken? Or whom have I defrauded? Whom have I oppressed? Or from whose hand have I taken a bribe to blind my eyes with it? Testify against me and I will restore it to you." They said, "You have not defrauded us or oppressed us or taken anything from any man's hand."*

13. Daniel 6:4. *Then the high officials and the satraps sought to find a ground for complaint against Daniel with regard to the kingdom, but they could find no ground for complaint or any fault, because he was faithful, and no error or fault was found in him.*

14. Genesis 39:6b-12. *So he left all that he had in Joseph's charge, and because of him he had no concern about anything but the food he ate. Now Joseph was handsome in form and appearance. And after a time his master's wife cast her eyes on Joseph and said, "Lie with me." But he refused and said to his master's wife, "Behold, because of me my master has no concern about anything in the house, and he has put everything that he has in my charge. He is not greater in this house than I am, nor has he kept back anything from me except you, because you are his wife. How then can I do this great wickedness and sin against God?" And as she spoke to Joseph day after day, he would not listen to her, to lie beside her or to be with her. But one day, when he went*

into the house to do his work, and none of the men of the house was there in the house, she caught him by his garment, saying, "Lie with me." But he left his garment in her hand and fled and got out of the house.

15. Joshua 1:6-9. *Be strong and courageous, for you shall cause this people to inherit the land that I swore to their fathers to give them. Only be strong and very courageous, being careful to do according to all the law that Moses my servant commanded you. Do not turn from it to the right hand or to the left, that you may have good success wherever you go. This Book of the Law shall not depart from your mouth, but you shall meditate on it day and night, so that you may be careful to do according to all that is written in it. For then you will make your way prosperous, and then you will have good success. Have I not commanded you? Be strong and courageous. Do not be frightened, and do not be dismayed, for the LORD your God is with you wherever you go."*

16. *Moreover, from the time that I was appointed to be their governor in the land of Judah, from the twentieth year to the thirty-second year of Artaxerxes the king, twelve years, neither I nor my brothers ate the food allowance of the governor. The former governors who were before me laid heavy burdens on the people and took from them for their daily ration forty shekels of silver. Even their servants lorded it over the people. But I did not do so, because of the fear of God.*

17. John 18:20. *Jesus answered him, "I have spoken openly to the world. I have always taught in synagogues and in the temple, where all Jews come together. I have said nothing in secret."*

18. Matthew 10:16. *"Behold, I am sending you out as sheep in the midst of wolves, so be wise as serpents and innocent as doves."*

19. John 14:6. *Jesus said to him, "I am the way, and the truth, and the life. No one comes to the Father except through me."*

20. I Corinthians 15: 14, 17. *We are even found to be misrepresenting God, because we testified about God that he raised Christ, whom he did not raise if it is true that the dead are not raised....And if Christ has not been raised, your faith is futile and you are still in your sins.*

21. I John 1:6. *If we say we have fellowship with him while we walk in darkness, we lie and do not practice the truth.*

22. II Corinthians 4:2. *But we have renounced disgraceful, underhanded ways. We refuse to practice cunning or to tamper with God's word, but by the open statement of the truth we would commend ourselves to everyone's conscience in the sight of God.*

23. Matthew 18:15-20. *"If your brother sins against you, go and tell him his fault, between you and him alone. If he listens to you, you have gained your brother. But if he does not listen, take one or two others along with you, that every charge may be established by the evidence of two or three witnesses. If he refuses to listen to them, tell it to the church. And if he refuses to listen even to the church, let him be to you as a Gentile and a tax collector. Truly, I say to you, whatever you bind on earth shall be bound in heaven, and whatever you loose on earth shall be loosed in heaven. Again I say to you, if two of you agree on earth about anything they ask, it will be done for them by my Father in heaven. For where two or three are gathered in my name, there am I among them."* I Corinthians 5:1-13.2b. *Let him who has done this be removed from among you.*

24. Ephesians 4:11. *And he gave the apostles, the prophets, the evangelists, the shepherds and teachers…*

25. Ephesians 3:10. *Sso that through the church the manifold wisdom of God might now be made known to the rulers and authorities in the heavenly places.*

26. Commander Kim, "Poll Finds Only 20% of Koreans Trust Protestant Church," *KoreaBang,* February 11, 2014. Downloaded fromchttp://www.koreabang.com/2014/stories/poll-finds-only-20-of-koreans-trust-protestant-church.html.

27. I Corinthians 5:13. *God judges those outside.*

28. Robert Mickens, "Can Pope Francis Succeed in Reforming the Curia?" *National Catholic Reporter,* May 26, 2015. Downloaded from http://ncronline.org/blogs/roman-observer/can-pope-francis-succeed-reformingcuria.

29. Tessa Wong, "Inside Singapore's City Harvest Church Megachurch Scandal," *BBC News*, October 21, 2015. Downloaded from http://www.bbc.com/news/world-asia-34589932.

30. Gary Short, *Animism in South Sudan*. Downloaded from http://www.hopeandgraceinternational.org/about-southern-sudan/animism-in-south-sudan/.

31. Ellis & Ter Haar, 156-57.

32. Matthew 16:18. *And I tell you, you are Peter, and on this rock will build my church, and the gates of hell shall not prevail against it.*

33. Micah 3:11. *Its heads give judgment for a bribe;*
its priests teach for a price;
its prophets practice divination for money;
yet they lean on the LORD and say,
"Is not the LORD in the midst of us?
No disaster shall come upon us."

34. The Christian Ethics Movement of Korea is one such organization that exists to challenge and correct the corruption within the Korean Protestant churches: http://cemk.org/2008/en/introduce.htm (English website address).

35. The "rulers and authorities in heavenly places" also refers to spiritual personalities (probably demons and angels) who are unseen but who have a limited role in affecting human affairs.

36. Deuteronomy 10:17. *For the LORD your God is God of gods and Lord of lords, the great, the mighty, and the awesome God, who is not partial and takes no bribe.*

37. Wise pastoral leaders know how to use good judgment on this matter.

38. See Chapter One.

39. Jeremiah 29: 7. *But seek the welfare of the city where I have sent you into exile, and pray to the Lord on its behalf, for in its welfare you will find your welfare.*

40. cf. I Corinthians 6:9-11. *Or do you not know that the unrighteous will not inherit the kingdom of God? Do not be deceived: neither the sexually immoral, nor idolaters, nor adulterers, nor men who practice homosexuality, nor thieves, nor the greedy, nor drunkards, nor revilers, nor swindlers will inherit the kingdom of God. And such were some of you. But you were washed, you were sanctified, you were justified in the name of the Lord Jesus Christ and by the Spirit of our God.* Colossians 3:5-11. *Put to death therefore what is earthly in you: sexual immorality, impurity, passion, evil desire, and covetousness, which is idolatry. On account of these the wrath of God is coming. In these you too once walked, when you were living in them. But now you must put them all away: anger, wrath, malice, slander, and obscene talk from your mouth. Do not lie to one another, seeing that you have put off the old self with its practices and have put on the new self, which is being renewed in knowledge after the image of its creator. Here there is not Greek and Jew, circumcised and uncircumcised, barbarian, Scythian, slave, free; but Christ is all, and in all.*

41. *Then God said, "Let us make man in our image, after our likeness. And let them have dominion over the fish of the sea and over the birds of the heavens and over the livestock and over all the earth and over every creeping thing that creeps on the earth."*
   So God created man in his own image,
      in the image of God he created him;
      male and female he created them.

   And God blessed them. And God said to them, "Be fruitful and multiply and fill the earth and subdue it, and have dominion over the fish of the sea and over the birds of the heavens and over every living thing that moves on the earth."

42. II Corinthians 5:17. *Therefore, if anyone is in Christ, he is a new creation. The old has passed away; behold, the new has come.*

43. Philippians 2:10-11. *So that at the name of Jesus every knee should bow, in heaven and on earth and under the earth, and every tongue confess that Jesus Christ is Lord, to the glory of God the Father.*

44. Eric Metaxas, *Amazing Grace: William Wilberforce and the Heroic Campaign to End Slavery* (San Francisco: HarperOne, 2007).

CHAPTER TWELVE

At the Foot of the Cross

"How do we transform the culture of corruption
into one of integrity and trust?"

As the collector and organizer of these various tales and interviews, I would like the final word.

The stories that fill this book are virtually a mirror of reality itself. It is an ugly reality that bruises our souls, aggravates our mistrust, exposes our shame, and makes us cry out, "What can be done about this terrible evil of massive, systemic corruption?"

We know the agony of a million—could it be 10 million or 50 million or 100 million? —daily defeats: Bribes passed, extortionists paid, millions of hours wasted because public officials will not do their job without a cash incentive, and email messages packed with lies sent to millions of readers around the globe. While thousands have died this day because of utter poverty and starvation, millions of corrupt officials, businesspeople, and their collaborators in various underground insurgencies and violent movements have filled their own stomachs, taken vacations, purchased luxury goods, and begun work on their second (or third, or even fourth) home abroad.

Because little pebbles of shame are buried in these stories, we may hop around in hopes that none of these pebbles handicaps our daily lives. We despise the corruption, but buried in our memories are those occasions when corruption benefited…us. It is hard to admit that in small but clever ways, we even took part in the evil system: We did not challenge when money was passed to the customs agent so that we could jump to the head of the long line of folks who couldn't afford to pay bribes. And there were those goods that we needed for God's work, and our friends slipped the funds under the table to liberate them from the port authorities. The litany of secret shame and lies is long, longer than we want to admit.

Corruption is a gloomy business that extracts value from society, whereas God designed humans to protect the earth and to produce what is needed so we can all flourish. Corruption, as we have seen, is a crushingly successful strategy of the Evil One, who works tirelessly to destroy humans rather than to let them flourish. Since it weaves its way through our lives and our societies, personal solutions are necessary, but insufficient. We also need solutions that undermine the systems that sustain it at the highest levels of government and business.

Note carefully: We are not political revolutionaries, for our strength is primarily spiritual. We take seriously the words of the Apostle Paul who reminded us that our battle is not against human beings, per se. Our battle is with an evil system that won't go away easily.[1]

We invite those who have extorted, cheated, and threatened us to meet at the common ground known as "the foot of the cross." There, together we will learn the answer to the question: "How do we transform the culture of corruption into a culture of integrity and trust?" That is, how do we truly tame the beast?

The answer we seek is personal enough to generate dramatic internal change and powerful enough to create a new culture where love for neighbors replaces lust for their possessions.

In my journeys about, I was fortunate to discover someone who truly understood the depth and breadth of the problem, and the divine capacity to tame and conquer it. What follows is my heavily edited account of that conversation, all of which I had to recall from memory. Unlike many of the earlier chapters, this can't be called a real interview; rather, it's my memoir of an interview that forever changed my life.

****

I met him on the road between the capital city and our medium-sized city two hours east. To avoid the bright sun, we sat down together under a tree with plates full of rice, some local meat (no, it wasn't the infamous bush meat of questionable origins), a bag of mangoes, and a big pot of tea.

He said he was a student of the Bible and a student of culture, and, yes, he had come back from his theological studies in North America to serve God back home. My concern was that his sojourn years ago in the land of Hollywood, Wall Street, and cowboys had dulled his love for his country and its people. I need not have worried.

You say that you have come here to serve. Please excuse my directness, but who, why, and how?

"I understand your caution," he said in reply. "We don't trust each other in this corrupt society, do we? " (He spoke without hesitation and the pretense that I usually associate with folks whose travels have led them to places I can only imagine visiting.)

The Bible student ignored my question and went on to suggest, "Wise people must make clear-minded assessments of their societies. Have we asked ourselves why we and our ancestors didn't mount a rebellion the first time a government official demanded a bribe for the licenses to drive autos, conduct business, build buildings, and so forth?"

I thought about it for a minute, and realized that he wasn't answering my questions, at least directly. He was the one who seemed to be the interrogator, and I had to answer him.

Could it be that we have always believed that those more powerful than us must be bribed so they don't hurt, but, instead, help us?

"Bingo!" he shouted, in the way that some Americans respond when you get the "right" answer to a question. "We little people think our role is to satisfy the 'big folks in our society." This constant effort to appease the powerful, whether humans or in the spiritual world, is called "works" in the Bible. "Bribes," he said, "are one way we work to get the powerful to help, not hurt us."

And then he asked: "Do you realize that once we start paying bribes, there is no end to it? The rich and powerful have no limits to their appetites. You work harder and harder, and pay bigger and bigger bribes to satisfy them. The strategy of 'works' is bound to fail."

(About that moment, a large snake slithered uncomfortably close. I froze for a minute, though my conversation partner carried on as if he had spent his entire life growing up around these reptilian creatures. I've tried hard to recall his comments during that 15-second interval when I sat stunned and a little afraid.)

I was fascinated by that comment. I had always thought the conversation about "works" was a conversation about the terms of salvation; I see now that the concept has vastly wider implications that, nevertheless, still validate the desperate need for redeeming grace.

What did you learn about this in your studies in America?

He laughed, and then suddenly started to choke on a big bite of food. After some more tea, he recovered and said, "Americans rarely talk about corruption unless it involves the occasional corrupt politician who usually makes a fool of himself and ends up in prison for his corruption."

(Yes, I said to myself, he *has* lived in the USA!)

Well, then, was there anything that you learned in America that could make sense of this massive beast called corruption?

"America's greatest strength was not its physical wealth, but its heritage of Christian faith. It is ridiculous for folks to talk about golden streets in America, because it's just not true." (I agreed, of course.) "But, what is true, " he said, "is that the earliest founders of what we know as the USA—they were called Puritans—believed that brutal honesty with God was absolutely essential. What made them honest was their intense willingness to ask a very painful question that we all ought to be asking ourselves.".

"Most American in those early days believed that the first thing they had to be honest about was the fact that their sinfulness deserved God's judgment." He learned in seminary that most Puritan prayers were constant reminders to God about how terribly sinful and corrupt they (the Puritans) were.[2] "That knowledge leveled the relationships between the rich and the poor, between the well-educated and the less-educated, between saint and sinner."

"And that knowledge," the student went on, "deeply humbled the brilliant Puritans who settled New England in hopes of establishing a society with functioning politics and what became over time a successful economy. They knew that universal corruption could kill the prospects for the young society in the harsh North American wilderness: The terrible risk was massive distrust, in which case no one would be able to buy and sell anything, because everyone would assume that the buyer or the seller was cheating them."

I was a little stunned to hear this. I always put my countrymen on a pedestal, and admired them, and what I heard from this man is that, at the beginning, everyone was humbled by the terrible, haunting reality of our fallen human condition. All they had was God. (See Chapter Nine for the example of an Asian nation that used a very different path to tame the beast of corruption.)

Well, what did they do about this problem?

"They came from Europe, " he said, "in search of religious freedom. Back home in England these Puritan clergy taught about the terrible sinfulness and personal corruption inside each of us, and the fact that God alone could do something about it. That message was unwelcome, but it is the message they brought with them to America in…"

Stop right there! Why in the world would God care about this problem?

"Because God is steadfast in His love for human beings," came the reply. "It is the most reliable love that the human race has ever known. The Hebrew word used in the Old Testament is *hesed*, which means a steady, loyal, undiminished love.

"God has that same love for human beings in this country, and in every country of the world. But we feel that the idea of God loving human beings is something very crude and inappropriate. Don't you agree?"

Okay, I agree. But, help me connect this to the problem of corruption right here.

"I'm coming back to what I was saying about those first Americans in the early 17th century. They knew that the one hope for the dreadful personal corruption that each of them carried to America—and that all of us carry around in ourselves at all times—is the death of Jesus Christ on the Cross 2000 years ago."

So, you are saying that the corrupt and those who suffer at their hands must appear together at the foot of the Cross of Christ?

"Bingo again!" came the reply. "All of us are in this together. For example, we all feel shame inside us when we pay or demand bribes. Those who engage in corruption want to hide their actions, just like the rest of us.

"The guilt and shame are resolved through the forgiveness that Christ offered when He gave His life on the Cross," he said. "You see, Jesus was God's Son and was perfectly sinless. The reason He died was to bear the punishment we should have borne for our corrupt souls, He took the punishment for us because He loved

212

us.[3]

"The solution to corruption starts inside of each of us, and none of us is too corrupt not to be forgiven and put on the path to new life because of His death. That's called 'Good News'!"

(By now we had eaten all our food, but, rather than feeling like I wanted an early afternoon rest, I was energized by the conversation. I had, however, shifted under a nearby tree, as the bright sun was burning my light skin.)

But, how does the Cross of Christ transform the corruption system that dominates societies around the world? I'm struggling to put the pieces together.

"I had little help with this while I was in North America. No one in the theological seminaries there talks or writes about this. And so I've wrestled by myself for years, and here is what I have concluded: You can only change, and ultimately tame, the corruption culture by changing the way you view God and how humans relate to Him.

"Let me explain," he went on. "I said earlier that we treat government officials like the way we treat the spirits: Pay them off so they do what you want them to do. I said that this kind of behavior means, in effect, you have to *do* something in order to get favorable action from either party. That system might seem fair until you realize that the large majority of the poor are completely left out, because they can't afford to pay what it takes for the official to give them a license for a business or to have regular electricity or whatever. The result is the rotten, destructive spoilage that characterizes our corrupt societies."

He continued to mention that the God who rules over the universe is completely different and operates with completely different rules. And, according to him, these rules are the ones that make for relatively successful, thriving societies like the USA.

So, how is God different and what are His rules? His reply was succinct: "First, God simply cannot be bribed. He won't take bribes. He doesn't want to be bribed. He hates bribes."[4]

What does that mean for the poor?

He was right to the point: "That means that they don't have to *do* something in order for God to do something for them. That means the poor can access justice, right?

"I elaborated about this earlier, remember? So rather than wanting something from us, like a bribe, God gives us something that we need, which is His love," he said.

He continued: "How did He do it? By showing us in the fullest possible way that humans can never approach God by giving Him something that He doesn't need; rather, He gives humans something we *desperately* need!"

What is that?

"We need three things, actually, but they all have to do with the one thing that makes God angry with humans: sin. First, we need to have someone forgive us of the terrible sin, including the greed, the selfishness, the injustice, the envy, the covetousness, the adulterous affairs inside our hearts. This resolves the terrible shame problem that I mentioned earlier. Secondly, we need to be reconciled to God and to our neighbors so that we can trust each other. Thirdly, we need to become people who once again undertake the responsibilities for which God designed us: to protect His creation and to produce what makes humans and the rest of creation flourish.

"And how did God deal with this so that we wouldn't have to pay a bribe or *do* something in order to satisfy these three deep needs?"

I would like to hear your answer to this question!

"He made His Son Jesus Christ die upon a Cross in Palestine about 2000 years ago, and when He did so He made Jesus bear the punishment for our sin, thus forgiving us, thus reconciling us, and thus making it possible for us to become new people who stop sinning and who start to protect and produce.[5] A culture that embraces this great story will be a culture where individuals are constantly adding value to their society so that the society advances and ultimately becomes rich. In contrast, a culture that is built upon bribing both spirits and government officials will destroy value, making their society poor. To put it simply, a corrupt society is a society that spoils, rots, and eventually dies."

He then referred to a professor from the University of California-Berkley who wrote about this as brilliantly as any human ever has:

> A bribe expresses self-interest; a gift conveys love. A bribe subordinates the recipient to the donor, a gift identifies the donor with the recipient. A gift brings no shame, a bribe must be in secret. A gift may be disclosed, a bribe must be concealed. The size of a gift is irrelevant; the size of a bribe, decisive. A gift does not oblige; a bribe coerces. A gift belongs to the donee; a bribe belongs to those to whom the bribe is accountable. [6]

The professor had more to say to this point:

> A chasm separates this uncoerced and uncoercive, loving, exemplary action [referring to the redemptive self-sacrifice of Jesus] from the manipulatively motivated, exploitative, secret exchange we call a bribe.[7]

"So," he went on, "Jesus gave His life as a self-sacrificial gift in order to restore our humanity to us, thus causing us to add value to life by becoming protectors and producers, rather than becoming extractors, through bribery and corruption, of the value that others have created.

"But, Jesus also achieved a great victory over the Devil and his minions, the demonic world. 'The reason the Son of God appeared was to destroy the works of the devil.'[8] In achieving a great victory over the Devil, Jesus also achieved a great victory over corruption. Everything that makes culture and society rot and spoil was destroyed, but most human beings, because they are personally corrupt and sinful, still live as if this victory is not real."

I felt myself overtaken, humbled by his blunt but brilliant answer to my question. Why hadn't anyone before explained so clearly this relationship between corruption, being human, and the death of Jesus Christ?

This is really powerful, but please explain the connection to taming the corruption system.

"Let me put it simply," said the young man who had so recently returned from theological studies in the USA. "Every time someone demands a bribe or extorts you, they act like the petty spirits that we are all afraid of or whose favor we try to buy. Every time a public official serves you without demanding a bribe, they are imitating the grace of the Supreme God of the Universe.

"How do most government officials want to be seen: as petty spirits, or the great God who rules over human affairs? I think the vast majority will choose the latter. How utterly tragic, then, when presidents and government officials act like petty spirits!

"But, why do so many act like the petty spirits? Many claim to be Christians, perhaps, but have never truly embraced the God who refuses bribes. When they truly follow Christ as the Son of God, they must refuse bribes because their God can't and won't take bribes under any circumstances! And, like the many Old Testament prophets, they become whistle-blowers who fearlessly announce the evil for what it is!"

This helps me a lot. I've never, ever thought about this problem in these terms. I think every pastor ought to preach this.

"A pastor who does so must first repent of his own complicity with corruption. And then he has to be absolutely clear that the problem of corruption is a universal human problem: Every one of us, by virtue of our sinfulness, is corrupt in our hearts, and if we don't embrace the same sense of personal sinfulness that the Puritans did, then the probability is that we will act in corrupt ways ourselves. And when citizens, not just government officials, are corrupt, then it has the same negative drag on the economy: We stay poor!

"So," he asked, "Are pastors ready to challenge their members about the products and services they sell at the market? Do they accurately represent what people are purchasing? What about property ownership? Is the pastor reminding people that land titles must be respected and honored by competent laws and courts? A sure and healthy sign of a restored nation is one where title deeds are recorded and witnessed, that is, there is transparency and clarity over matters of property ownership."[9]

I saw the implications. He went on: "Why don't citizens hold their public officials accountable when they break the law? Shouldn't pastors empower their members to do so, since everyone benefits when lawbreakers are properly punished? That includes insisting that they make restitution for what they have stolen.[10]

"Pastors must teach that the stories we teach our children will shape their moral imaginations, for good or for ill. Why is that in some societies the stories told to young children involve clever, sly animals who steal and maim? Will not children grow up to do likewise, perhaps as corrupt officials?

"Do pastors and religious leaders teach their people to repent?[11] Repentance means a complete change of direction, a complete change of mind, about corruption. When John the Baptist 'proclaimed a baptism of repentance for the forgiveness of sins:'[12]

> The crowds asked him, "What then shall we do?" And he answered them, "Whoever has two tunics is to share with him who has none, and whoever has food is to do likewise." Tax collectors also came to be baptized and said to him, "Teacher, what shall we do?" And he said to them, "Collect no more than you are authorized to do." Soldiers also asked him, "And we, what shall we do?" And he said to them, "Do not extort money from anyone by threats or by false accusation, and be content with your wages."[13]

"Perhaps some religious leaders will have to begin repenting themselves. Many enjoy the fruits of corruption either because there is corruption inside their churches or because they do not want to offend corrupt officials and businesspeople who are major donors. Religious leaders are impotent on this issue unless they repent and turn from the wicked ways that they would otherwise publicly condemn."

What about those who have no exposure to Jesus Christ: What do I say to them?

"Our Muslim friends face an agonizing reality," he said. "Five out of ten of the most corrupt nations in the world have an Islamic culture of some kind. Something is tragically wrong, and Western nations can't be blamed for this. Their solution is to submit to God as His slave, but it never transforms our corrupt inner disposition.

"I want my Muslim friends to realize that there is only one basis for approaching God, and that is *grace*, which means letting God give you a gift, as opposed to *doing* something for Him. Cultures that make *doing* to satisfy God will not produce the trust, the self-giving love, the determination to produce value rather than extract it, and the legal culture that makes economies thrive. There is only one effective way to implant these characteristics in the culture, and that is through embracing Jesus Christ as God's gift to us: forgiving us of sin, reconciling us with God and our neighbor, and letting God transform our motives. Instead of corrupt value extractors, we become virtuous value adders who protect His creation and produce what makes humans and the rest of creation thrive and flourish.

"By the way, our friends in Buddhist and Hindu societies also have terrible problems with corruption. Part of their deep problem is that their monistic[14] worldview destroys the real distinctions between what is good and what is bad. On the other hand, they have the same basic problem as the Muslims: *Doing* something in order to achieve their goal, *nirvana*, rather than letting God do for them what they can never do for themselves."

What about people in societies that for many decades have been deeply shaped by Marxist ideas?

"They have shaped a lot of Western thinkers who want to improve society without God. That was their fatal error: They thought that they could build a moral system out of pure matter, because they believe matter is all there is. But, the effort is utterly hopeless. Rocks don't produce morality, do they?!

"So, people from Marxist societies have no fundamental, purely moral reason why corruption is wrong. All they know is that corruption is destroying the souls of their societies and making people powerless. My advice to them from our little roadside rendezvous: Turn to God in order to know why corruption is wrong and to find His solution to the problem. The Marxist has to meet us, along with the Muslim, Buddhist, Hindu, and others, at the same place: the foot of the Cross."

It's been a long afternoon, but one that I will never forget. I have one final question: Are there practical steps that citizens can take in order to transform the culture of corruption into one of integrity and trust?

"I think that every pastor or religious leader needs to start talking about this problem in the terms that I just defined it. This could create a slowly expanding revolution of integrity in our countries. People will need patience, perseverance and courage to start something new, but God will aid them as they step out in faith and trust. Selfishness and sin will always exist, but communities that offer care, justice and true freedom will attract both weary sinners and the sinned-against to work together.

"Remind followers of Christ that corruption belongs in their *past* lives, never in the present. They should teach that corruption violates our dignity as God's image bearers and violates our human purpose as virtuous protectors and producers. Finally, they can show that only through the sinless Son of God, Jesus Christ, is God able to create in each of us a new heart that is oriented toward the virtue of love for neighbors and away from the vice of corruption.

"A philosopher encouraged people to work with God because of the joy they find:

> By relying on his word and presence we are enabled to reintegrate the little realm that makes up our life into the infinite rule of God. And that is the eternal kind of life. Caught up in his active rule, our deeds become an element in God's eternal history. They are what God and we do

At the Foot of the Cross

together, making us part of his life and his a part of ours.[15]

"James Yen was a remarkable American-educated Chinese educator who was surrounded by local and national corruption in early to mid 20th century China. His wife once commented, 'The driving force which has brought this movement through such difficulties and heavy odds stems from Jim's deep conviction from the start that this work is not his, but God's.'[16] Study his life and that of others like him. He was once a foreign student in America (1916-20), and he returned home as a Christ-animated agent of change.

"Beyond that, I have dozens of ideas that I have been working on for years. Some of these I discussed with other international students while I was abroad. Would you agree to share these with the rest of the world?" (I have attached his list of practical ideas as an appendix to this book.)

Most certainly. Thank you for an afternoon I will never forget.

"Let's get out there and tame the beast, shall we?"

SUMMARY

1. Resisting corruption and creating a culture of integrity depends on realizing:
   a. God's loving concern for humans and their societies.
   b. All of us suffer from a deep propensity to inner corruption (sin).
   c. Jesus Christ was the perfect sacrifice who bore the punishment for our corruption so that He can:
      i. Forgive us.
      ii. Reconcile us to Him and to one another.
      iii. Make us new people who reject the corruption culture.
   d. His design for the human race is a culture of grace that adds value by protecting and producing, rather than human efforts to achieve *nirvana*, forced

redistribution, and submitting to God as his slave.

e. By resisting corruption and creating a culture of grace we participate in Christ's victory over the Devil.

2. Pastors must be prepared to teach this to their congregations:
    a. Offer practical strategies for taming the beast of corruption.
    b. Point to real life examples of those who were courageous Christian change agents.

STUDY GUIDE

1. How does the young theologian's message connect the concern for personal salvation with conquering corruption?
2. Why is grace so central to his ideas?
3. What biblical verses best illustrate his main points?
4. Why are the Muslim, Marxist, and Eastern religious approaches inadequate to the task of taming the beat of corruption?
5. With whom will you share this book, making sure to schedule a follow-up conversation to discuss its implications?
6. What practical idea for "Taming the Beast" (found in the Appendix) will you and your group employ as a result of reading this chapter?

NOTES

1. Ephesians 6:12. *For we do not wrestle against flesh and blood, but against the rulers, against the authorities, against the cosmic powers over this present darkness, against the spiritual forces of evil in the heavenly places.*

2. e.g., A.G. Bennett, *The Valley of Vision: A Collection of Puritan Prayers and Devotions* (Carlisle, PA: Banner of Truth, 2003). cf. Catherine A. Brekus, *Sarah Osborn's World* (New Haven, CT: Yale University Press, 2013).

3. II Corinthians 5:19. *that is, in Christ God was reconciling the world to himself, not counting their trespasses against them, and entrusting to us the message of reconciliation.* II Corinthians 5:21. *For our sake he made him to be sin who knew no sin, so that in him we might become the righteousness of God.*

4. Deuteronomy 10:17. *For the LORD your God is God of gods and Lord of lords, the great, the mighty, and the awesome God, who is not partial and takes no bribe.*

5. Colossians 1:19. *For in him all the fullness of God was pleased to dwell.,* Colossians 2:13-14. *And you, who were dead in your trespasses and the uncircumcision of your flesh, God made alive together with him, having forgiven us all our trespasses, by canceling the record of debt that stood against us with its legal demands. This he set aside, nailing it to the cross.*

6. John T. Noonan, Jr., *Bribes* (New York: Macmillan, 1984), 697.

7. Noonan, 696.

8. I John 3:8. *"The wind blows where it wishes, and you hear its sound, but you do not know where it comes from or where it goes. So it is with everyone who is born of the Spirit."*

9. Jeremiah 32:44. *"Fields shall be bought for money, and deeds shall be signed and sealed and witnessed, in the land of Benjamin, in the places about Jerusalem, and in the cities of Judah, in the cities of the hill country, in the cities of the Shephelah, and in the cities of the Negeb; for I will restore their fortunes, declares the LORD."*

10. Numbers 5:5-10. *And the LORD spoke to Moses, saying, "Speak to the people of Israel, When a man or woman commits any of the sins that people commit by breaking faith with the LORD, and that person realizes his guilt, he shall confess his sin that he has committed. And he shall make full restitution for his wrong, adding a fifth to it and giving it to him to whom he did the wrong. But if the man has no next of kin to whom restitution may be made for the wrong, the restitution for wrong shall go to the LORD for the priest, in addition to the ram of atonement with which atonement is made for him. And every contribution, all the holy donations of the people of Israel,*

which they bring to the priest, shall be his. Each one shall keep his holy donations: whatever anyone gives to the priest shall be his."

11. e.g., Acts 3:19. *Repent therefore, and turn back, that your sins may be blotted out.*

12. Luke 3:3. *And he went into all the region around the Jordan, proclaiming a baptism of repentance for the forgiveness of sins.*

13. Luke 3:10-14. *And the crowds asked him, "What then shall we do?" And he answered them, "Whoever has two tunics is to share with him who has none, and whoever has food is to do likewise." Tax collectors also came to be baptized and said to him, "Teacher, what shall we do?" And he said to them, "Collect no more than you are authorized to do." Soldiers also asked him, "And we, what shall we do?" And he said to them, "Do not extort money from anyone by threats or by false accusation, and be content with your wages."*

14. This means that everything is one.

15. Dallas Willard, *The Divine Conspiracy* (San Francisco: Harper Row, 1998), 27.

16. Stacey Bieler, "James Yen," in C. L. Hamrin & S. Bieler (Eds.), *Salt and Light: Lives of Faith that Shaped Modern China (Volume 1)* (Eugene, OR: Wipf & Stock, 2009), 118.

Conclusion

Taming the beast called corruption brings us to the Cross where Jesus Christ gave His life not only for those tempted by it, but for those who also succumb.

What kind of life follows? We already know that societies where corruption is rare are noted for their high levels of trust and prosperous economies. But, what does Jesus promise to the person who renounces corruption in favor of a life of honesty and integrity?

Jesus painted a picture of this new life when he preached the Beatitudes found in Matthew 5:2-11. To paraphrase His words in the context of our passion to end corruption:

1. If you suffer poverty, corrupt wealth is utterly inferior to living under God's eternal rule and reign (v. 3: *Blessed are the poor in spirit, for theirs is the kingdom of heaven*).

2. If you must suffer loss in your pursuit of an honest life, your sorrows will always be met by the comforting, encouraging friendship of those you have treated kindly and honestly (v. 4: *Blessed are those who mourn, for they shall be comforted*).

3. Though you could manipulate people with your money, how much greater is the restrained use of your power ("meek") for others' good; the result will be that people will demand that you become their leader ("inherit the earth") (v. 5: *Blessed are the meek, for they shall inherit the earth*).

4. Whereas greed and corruption are never satisfied, the deep, passionate desire for justice and holiness always satisfies, day after day (v. 6: *Blessed are those who hunger and thirst for righteousness, for they shall be satisfied*).

5. Rather than making demands for bribes, showing mercy and kindness to people makes them want to shower you with the same mercy and kindness (v. 7: *Blessed are the merciful, for they shall receive mercy*).

6. Those who are not corrupt have nothing to hide, and will not only never fear others but also never fear the face of God (v. 8: *Blessed are the pure in heart, for they shall see God*).

7. Those who help others to be reconciled with each other will be wealthy beyond imagination, for as God's children they will inherit the wealth of His kingdom (v. 9: *Blessed are the peacemakers, for they shall be called sons of God*).

8. If, in your pursuit of godliness, the corrupt make your life miserable, remember what the poor person knows so very well: Nothing can compare with the glories of living under God's rule and reign (v. 10: *Blessed are those who are persecuted for righteousness' sake, for theirs is the kingdom of heaven*).

9. If you are mercilessly attacked for living a life of honesty and purity, take great joy in two facts: 1) The Old Testament prophets suffered similarly, and that means you are in good company; and 2) You will have a greater reward than the richest corrupt leader could ever imagine (vv. 11-12: *Blessed are you when others revile you and persecute you and utter all kinds of evil against you falsely on my account. Rejoice and be glad, for your reward is great in heaven, for so they persecuted the prophets who were before you*).

Go forth in courage, inspired and empowered by Jesus Christ to tame the beast of corruption. This scourge deserves to die, and, when it does, nations—and you and your family and your community—will rejoice.

Appendix

PRACTICAL STRATEGIES FOR TAMING THE BEAST

Students
1. Begin student groups and campus clubs that conduct studies about and create strategies for conquering corruption.
2. Create competitions that reward students who develop the most promising solutions to corruption.
3. Undertake student essay contests on the questions "The True Costs of Corruption" and "How Do We End Corruption?"
4. Watch films about corruption (e.g., the 2014 Russian film *Leviathan*), and then convene discussion groups that explore why corruption is so pervasive and what needs to be done to stop it.
5. Develop student-led websites and social networking platforms for a student-driven initiative to end corruption.

Government
1. Form accountability groups for government employees under great pressure to participate in corrupt activities.
2. Develop laws that require politicians and upper level government employees to make full disclosure of their wealth and property. This transparency will go a long ways to building trust and confidence.
3. Develop an advisory board of religious leaders who are specifically authorized to report to the media evidence of official corruption.
4. Temporary lending agencies need to provide partial loan assistance for low-level government officials who are not paid timely salaries. They will repay loans when salaries are finally paid.
5. Develop *compensatory funding mechanisms* (CFMs) that will for a given period of time (perhaps five or ten years) provide

supplementary funding to ethnic communities, or tribes, who refuse to insist on their "time to eat." That is, if groups renounce traditional demands for special hiring favors, kickbacks, and other corrupt mechanisms for using government funds to favor their ethnic groups at the expense of other groups, they will receive a special distribution from the government. In addition, the government will train teachers in those communities to implement an anti-corruption curriculum (see below under "Education").

Churches/Religious institutions

1. Discipline members who participate in acts of corruption and who refuse to repent after regular admonitions to do so.
2. When fellow Christians become involved in disputes involving corrupt acts, provide a venue for dispute resolution.
3. In collaboration with national and international associations of churches, create *corruption amelioration funds* (CAF) that provide financial assistance to members who suffer directly because they are not willing to participate in corruption.
   a. Standards of proof will need to be established, along with methods for examining the evidence of material harm caused by corruption.
   b. Liability will need to be limited, which means that the fund will only cover, say, 50% of the legitimate loss due to resisting corruption.
   c. The fund risks becoming corrupt if established institutional checks and balances that limit the decision-making power of any single individual are not established. In addition, regular audits must be conducted by reputable international auditing agencies.
   d. This needs to be backed up by an international reinsurance fund that will help to insure countrywide *corruption amelioration funds* when faced with heavy claims that threaten the viability of the

fund.

4. Pastors can preach and teach regularly about corruption.

5. Educational materials about how to confront and deal with this topic can be created for use in local churches

6. Support groups can be created for those who have renounced corruption and who need regular encouragement from others who also were once active in corruption.

7. Institute annual "End Corruption/Promote Integrity" Sundays, during which church members will be invited to make "No Bribe" pledges: "I will neither give nor receive bribes."

8. Pastors may refuse communion to those who engage in bribery and corruption and who remain unrepentant.

9. Develop national associations of pastoral leaders who commit to preach against and fight corruption in their countries.

10. Seminaries and Bible colleges can develop coursework on corruption, bribery, and extortion.

11. Ask networks of Western churches to appeal to their governments to enforce their own anti-corruption laws, thus making it difficult for corrupt, non-Western government officials to hide corrupt funds in Western institutions (see below under "International").

12. Bribe Box: If someone asks for a bribe, then the church member anonymously puts the name of the corrupt official in the "bribe box" at church. When the same name appears at least five times, then church leaders have sufficient evidence to approach the government with a meaningful accusation against the public official.

13. Form an international church network wherein Western churches provide refuge for those who suffer for their attack on corruption.

14. Develop "truth commissions" that research the extent of corruption within churches, and then call out church leaders to repent for allowing this evil to persist within their churches and denominations.

Appendix

Business

1. Explore, then join the remarkable global initiative founded in South Africa called Unashamedly Ethical: *http://unashamedlyethical.com/*. This organization has rallied more than 5000 business and other leaders across the globe to a campaign for ethics, values, and clean living. They urge absolute transparency and honesty in contracting and other business relationships.

2. Creatively employ an asset-based development model with those who regularly demand bribes:

    a. Example: Extortionists demand money to protect a successful business, with the implied threat that they will destroy the business if they are not regularly paid.

    b. Hypothetical response: *"I am so very glad to see you! I have been waiting for you, and in fact I have been praying for you. May I offer you and your colleagues a better proposal, one that will restore your honor in the society while also putting you on the path to legitimate employment so that your families can be healthy and prosperous? There will be some conditions, such as the willingness to work hard, but I have no doubt that you and many of your colleagues will relish this proposal.*

    "I want to employ several of your people in my business, but in order to come onto my payroll, they must be hard workers who do their very best. So, I propose that you ask your colleagues to enter a competition in order to discover which two of them can produce the finest product (or service). I will then hire those two, and pay them a fine salary. Since the Bible teaches that tithing is an appropriate way to share wealth, they can distribute 10% of their earnings with the rest of the group. If they do a fine job, and our business grows, then we will want to hire more of your people.

    "Not only that, I want you and your colleagues to be trained in business development so that you learn what God says about business development. I will train your people in biblical principles of healthy business development, and then

230

you will join us on a team of business educators who will train the rest of your people how to start successful businesses that make their families prosperous and very honorable. You, of course, will have the greatest honor, because through you they will learn this valuable education.

"Every thing we do, I am sure you can imagine, will involve seeking to please God. Shall we pray about this idea together? Why don't we meet tomorrow and begin to implement this plan? I will look forward to working with you so that you not only gain great esteem as a creative leader, but your families will start to flourish through hard work."

3. Form accountability groups for businesspersons who face demands to participate in corrupt activities.
4. Teach businesspeople to ask these questions when asked for special payments:
   a. Is it lawful?
   b. Is the deal transparent to all parties?
   c. Does the action reflect the Golden Rule: Do unto others, as you would have them do to you?
   d. Does anyone involved feel uncomfortable about what is proposed?

Leadership
1. Preach and teach Exodus 18:21 as the standard for church and public leadership
2. Encourage religious leaders to meet with government officials and ask them to end institutionalized corruption.
3. Advocate for legal compensation increases for government officials, accompanied by an increase in taxes to pay for this. This should be accompanied by the employment of a government financial manager that can manage cash flow so that government employees are paid on time. (Bribery must be described as informal taxation.)
4. Create annual awards for the least corrupt public officials, including legislators, bureaucrats, as well as specific offices. This requires an excellent investigative process.

5. Consider whistleblower awards.
6. Explore, as a model, the Malaysian-based anti-corruption initiative *Oriental Hearts and Mind Study Institute,* which in September 2014 sponsored the 7th National Congress on Integrity.

Media

1. Develop YouTube videos of actual acts of corruption.
2. Develop plays and other artistic media that highlight the tragedy of corruption.
   a. What about a creative adaptation of Jesus' cleansing the Jewish temple as a story about Jesus driving out the bribe-takers and corrupt officials?
   b. Create humorous skits that ridicule the corruption culture and the practices that sustain it.
3. Create "bribing stations," that is, officially designated centers, or buildings where all bribes must take place (as a means of shaming both bribe givers and takers).
4. Create smartphone apps:
   a. To record and promote videos of actual corruption.
   b. To host a library of anti-corruption lessons that can be shown to adults and children.
   c. That list all the anti-corruption references in the Bible, along with short commentary.

Education

1. Develop K-12 curricula that teach about citizen rights and laws regarding corruption.
2. Create parent education program where parents are taught new nursery rhymes, stories, parables that promote integrity.
3. Devise evangelistic preaching and appeals that are attuned to the phenomenon of corruption, including a "Four Spiritual Laws for Those in Corrupt Societies."
4. Develop civil society-based monitoring and research organization to raise public consciousness of the problem.
5. Develop appropriate advertising strategies that involve traditional advertising venues, such as billboards, TV ads,

etc.

6. Conduct fortnightly public roundtables where citizens report their experiences with corruption and bribery.
7. Seek research funding to understand the many cultural, as well as institutional and structural variables that contribute to the culture of corruption.
8. Create support groups for those who are berated and attacked on the job for their resistance to corruption.
9. Invite academic researchers to study the common ways that people participate in corruption: evading taxes, paying bribes, extorting others, etc.

Legal
1. Use grand juries to develop cases against corruption.
2. Capitalize upon existing Christian justice initiatives (e.g., International Justice Mission) that could be invited to enlarge their arenas of operation to include bribery, corruption, and extortion.

International
1. Create a sustained international network of anti-corruption campaigners.
2. Create an international protection fund to help those who need refuge and protection when they expose corruption
3. Promote and create educational materials around the *United Nations Declaration against Corruption and Bribery in International Commercial* *Transactions:* http://www.un.org/documents/ga/res/51/a51r191.htm
4. Promote current international campaigns against corruption:
   a. UNODC's Action against Corruption and Economic Crime: https://www.unodc.org/unodc/en/corruption/
   b. I Paid a Bribe.com: An Indian-based website that invites people to report bribes demanded and those paid: *www.Ipaidabribe.com*
   c. Others

Appendix

Contribute Your Ideas to a Global Movement

The beast, as we have been calling the culture of corruption, is a monster that consumes lives while simultaneously debilitating and sometimes destroying whole societies. We believe, however, that Jesus Christ, as Sovereign King over the Universe, wants to tame the beast. We also believe that He wants to use people like you to be part of his "team of tamers."

Please go to *www.wilberforceacademy.org/corruption* and share (anonymously) your ideas, stories, videos, or photos for successfully reigning in corruption. Don't be shy! Share.

Made in the USA
Lexington, KY
24 March 2017